MW01124327

Praise for *Together We...*

Abraham Chen is a warm-hearted servant of the living God. Through the ups and downs of pastoral ministry, Chen shows us an example of fervent love of God, and he also shows us our great God, faithful, powerful, and immanent. Richly illustrated with personal stories, these sermons will warm your heart as well.

—Jeffrey Arthurs
Professor of Preaching and Communication
Gordon-Conwell Theological Seminary

Pastor Abraham Chen, a spiritual educator, teaches us in his sermons that "Each of us should look not only to our own interests, but also to the interests of others." As a secular educator myself, I agree with it whole heartedly. With God's blessing, an educator is able to attend to the interests of students who have varied social, ethnic and religious background with no reservation.

—Chung Nan Chang
President
Chu Hai College of Higher Education

Abraham Chen has compiled a book of sermons that will serve the body of Christ both as a model for the excellent use of Scripture in expository preaching for pastors and ministers, and also as a manual for the lay person who wants to passionately pursue God in holiness while making a difference as an active member of his/her church and community. Abraham is refreshingly honest and humble, effectively weaving the triumphs and tragedies of his own journey into his sermons as illustrations of his exegesis as he transfers his sound biblical preaching from the pulpit to the printed page.

Abraham provides a window into his own personal and spiritual pilgrimage as a way of challenging men and women to be prayerful, joyful, committed, resilient, consistent disciples of Jesus Christ. He draws from his difficult pre-Christian childhood in Taiwan, his formative years as a young seminarian, his joys and sorrows as a church planter and pastor, and his missionary travels around the world. You will learn much from both his successes and his failures, and you will be given many tools that will point you to Jesus and equip you for more faithful service in fulfillment of the Great Commission. I commend *Together We ... Sermons for Advancing the Gospel* to you as a moving and compelling exercise that will enhance your homiletical and devotional aspirations, to the glory of God.

—David Cole
VP of Student Development and Pastoral Care
Assistant Professor of Theology
Briercrest College and Seminary

These sermons are deep and insightful, filled with faith and an inspiring new perspective on overcoming adversity and finding a way to triumph.

—Tony Evans
Senior Pastor of Oak Cliff Bible Fellowship

Pastor Chen's sermons will inspire any reader through his winsome stories and biblical insights. Through these sermons we get a glimpse of God's encouraging work through a pastor and in his people, the church.

—Scott M. Gibson
Haddon W. Robinson Professor of Preaching and Ministry
Director of the Haddon W. Robinson Center for Preaching
Gordon-Conwell Theological Seminary

This is a delightful book of sermons. Each is well illustrated and relevant to today's needs. The stories chosen are interesting and well suited to each subject. These are real sermons that were preached to the congregation of the Fountain of Joy Prayer Church in San Jose. They cover such topics as humility, faith, prayer in the Spirit, witnessing, and praise.

Many of the illustrations come from Pastor Chen's own life experience. He has not been afraid to expose some of the difficult situations that he himself has faced, and he shows how God met every one of his needs.

This is a book I highly recommend to be read prayerfully and thoughtfully. It will inspire the reader to draw closer to God.

—Dr. Roy Hayden
Old Testament Professor at Kings University

Abraham has a heart for God and a heart for people. And his heart—shared openly and humbly—will touch your heart for God as well.

—John Ortberg
Bestselling author and pastor
The Life You've Always Wanted: Spiritual Growth for Ordinary People

No richer ministry is birthed than when it emerges from the edges of organizational death mixed with the brokenness of a leader's life. Abraham Chen's epistle to his Fountain of Joy Prayer Church presents a portfolio of spiritual perspective, biblical citation, personal vignette, and contemporary illustration—all ingredients of a faithful pulpit ministry. His desire to preach and teach preaching as the health-source of a spiritually growing church will resonate with all who believe that as pastors take care of church health, God takes care of church growth. May God's Spirit use God's servants like Pastor Abraham Chen to deliver God's Word to grow God's church to reach God's world for God's glory.

—Ramesh Richard
President, Ramesh Richard Evangelism and Church Health [RREACH]
Founder & Chair, Trainers of Pastors International Coalition [TOPIC]
Professor of Pastoral Ministries and Global Theological Engagement
Dallas Theological Seminary

Abraham is brimming over with joy and love for others. Not only did I experience that in seminary but now in his writings. It is an exuberance that catches one by surprise. I can see him pressing on, even when most of his congregants left. Nothing would stop him from walking in faith, loving others and doing what he deeply feels call to do: minister Christ's grace to all he touches. This you too will feel as you read.

—Brian C Stiller
Past President
Tyndale University College & Seminary

For years, lay pastors have been looking for ways to upgrade and to enrich their preaching. And now, by God's grace, a long-awaited book has appeared: *Together We ... Sermons for Advancing the Gospel.*

According to Pastor Chen's own testimony, both the afflictions of his younger years in Taiwan and the trials of the early part of his ministry in the United States have served as God's crucible in the formation of his growth and maturity.

May this book be greatly used by the Lord as a help to laity and leaders alike in the interpretation and the deliverance of God's Word to this spiritually impoverished world today.

—Thomas Wang
President emeritus
Great Commission International

Chen's book is a joy to read and a refreshment to the soul. It is said that a person with an experience is no match for a person with an argument, but when you combine experience, with knowledge, and add passion as Chen does in this book you have a powerful insightful document. Chen's book is a must read for every Christian, whether enjoying the mountain top or walking through the valley. Chen uses appropriate examples to illustrate his points and writes in a clear, concise, enjoyable style. I encourage you to read the book now.

—Bruce E. Winston
Dean, School of Global Leadership & Entrepreneurship
Regent University

TOGETHER WE...

TOGETHER WE...

Sermons for Advancing the Gospel

Abraham Chen

WinePressPublishing
Great Books, Defined.

© 2011 by Abraham Chen. All rights reserved.

WinePress Publishing (PO Box 428, Enumclaw, WA 98022) functions only as the book publisher. As such, the ultimate design, content, editorial accuracy, and views expressed or implied in this work are those of the author.

No part of this publication may be reproduced, stored in a retrieval system or transmitted in any way by any means—electronic, mechanical, photocopy, recording, or otherwise—without the prior permission of the copyright holder, except as provided by USA copyright law.

Unless otherwise noted, all Scriptures are taken from the *Holy Bible, New International Version*®, *NIV*®. Copyright © 1973, 1978, 1984 by Biblica, Inc.™ Used by permission of Zondervan. All rights reserved worldwide. www. zondervan.com

ISBN 13: 978-1-60615-188-4
ISBN 10: 1-60615-188-6
Library of Congress Catalog Card Number: 2010933045

To Fountain of Joy Prayer Church

CONTENTS

FOREWORD

Abraham Chen goes hard after God. He also has a deep love and concern for his people. He believes in the centrality of prayer and the strategic force of biblical preaching. This collection of sermons reflects those passions in Abraham's soul.

Sermons written, however, are never the same as sermons preached. Sermons on the page cannot convey the heat, the tears, or the heart of the preacher like sermons from a pulpit. Written sermons can be more precise and the paragraphs more measured, and that benefits the reader. Yet as you read these sermons you can sense that they are not literary contributions, but the attempt to capture the power of a pulpit and put it down in writing.

I thank God for every attempt to advance the cause of relevant, biblical preaching. For that reason I commend Abraham Chen and these sermons to you.

Haddon Robinson
Harold John Ockenga Professor of Preaching
Gordon Conwell Theological Seminary

PREFACE

I first began working on this book at the gentle prodding of Professor Haddon W. Robinson, who was my doctoral program mentor and adviser. Thanks to the love of my family and fellow Christians at Fountain of Joy Prayer Church, my labors have, at long last, borne fruit. Though not part of my church, Dr. Robinson has given generous support and encouragement to my work, and I would like to offer him my heartfelt thanks.

It has been my particular desire over the years to teach lay people, or lay pastors, to preach expository sermons. My prayer has always been that one day I would be able to use Dr. Robinson's textbook in my teaching—with my own sermons serving as examples of his methods in actual practice.

I also hope ordinary men and women who are simply searching for grace and truth will find in these sermons a source of spiritual insight into how the Lord is indeed faithful and full of mercy. Having experienced God's amazing grace, I feel obligated to share it with others. And if this collection of sermons contributes in some small measure to bringing others to Christ, I will consider my time in preparing it to have been well spent.

Now I want you to know, brothers, that what has happened to me has really served to advance the gospel. As a result, it has become clear throughout the whole palace guard and to everyone else that I am in chains for Christ. Because of my chains, most of the brothers in the Lord have been encouraged to speak the word of God more courageously and fearlessly. It is true that some preach Christ out of envy and rivalry, but others out of goodwill. The latter do so in love, knowing that I am put here for the defense of the gospel. The former preach Christ out of selfish ambition, not sincerely, supposing that they can stir up trouble for me while I am in chains. But what does it matter? The important thing is that in every way, whether from false motives or true, Christ is preached. And because of this I rejoice.

—Philippians 1:12–18

Chapter 1

TOGETHER WE ADVANCE THE GOSPEL

On the final day of the "Doing Church as a Team" conference, featuring keynote speaker Pastor Wayne Cordeiro from Hawaii, we received mini flashlights—apparently as a token of appreciation. We thanked the conference manager for his thoughtfulness. We later learned, however, that they were more than just small gifts. Pastor Wayne turned off all the lights and asked us to turn on our flashlights. In the darkness, the pastor asked how many of us were full-time ministers. A few people raised their hands, flashlights gleaming. Pastor Wayne explained the biblical concept of being a full-time minister. Only then did we all remember that *everyone* is called to be a full-time minister. After his talk, Pastor Wayne asked the same question again, and everyone present raised a flashlight! When we saw those lights illuminating the dark room, it was a powerful representation of full-time ministry in a dark world. With flashlights lit and raised high, we all sang, "But as for me and my household, we will serve the Lord."

Everyone Is Called

We should rejoice to declare the praises of him who called us out of darkness into his wonderful light (1 Pet. 2:9). Yes! We all will rejoice

1

in the mission and make Christ known. We all will tell people of the gospel: "That Christ died for our sins according to the Scriptures, that he was buried, that he was raised on the third day according to the Scriptures" (1 Cor. 15:3–4). Some of you are teachers, some are social workers, some are doctors, and some are ministers or pastors. No matter what profession you are in, no matter what your status or age or background, you can still minister God's Word so long as you are obeying God's will for you.

When I was studying geology and archeology in Israel, I heard of an elderly gentleman who gave his heart to Christ when he was seventy years old. He preached to us at a tiny chapel on Mount Carmel where Elijah encountered the false prophets. One is never too old to preach the gospel! Young children can touch our hearts and bring us to Christ as well. The other day, I watched a powerful story on YouTube™ about Logan Henderson, a thirteen-year-old boy who lives on a ranch in a tiny town in Nebraska. Logan listens to a Christian radio station regularly. One day, he called the station because he was very distraught and wanted to tell his story to everyone listening. He started by saying he did not understand why God would let his calf's back be broken. Even though the calf was special to him, Logan had had to kill it himself. Confused, he asked God this question and he heard God say, "You know, Logan, my Son was special, but he died for a purpose."

"It's kind of the same thing: that calf was close to me and God's Son was close to him, but I just wanted to tell you guys that it's so important," Logan said, describing faith. "Just remember that when you lose a loved one or a pet, know that God gave his Son too, and that he understands. He will always understand. He always will, just run to him."[1] Logan showed wisdom beyond his age. Since Logan's story aired, the phone call and the video clip have taken on a life of their own. People from all around the world have watched and been inspired.

You can be another Logan. God could have called the angels to rescue people, but in his eternal plan, the lost are to be saved through us—through every one of us. You are as important as Billy Graham or Mother Teresa.

In Every Way Christ Is Preached

No one served the Lord as insightfully as the apostle Paul. When he was imprisoned in Rome, Paul wrote to the Philippians describing the great secret he learned. Though he was in jail for preaching the gospel, he continued his efforts, because being jailed itself advanced his gospel. When all the people from the palace guard to his own followers learned he was imprisoned for Christ, they were emboldened to spread the Good News themselves.

Paul was someone who could turn even being thrown in jail into an advantage for the cause of Christ. Likewise, when some preached God's Word through envy and rivalry, Paul merely said: "But what does it matter? The important thing is that in every way, whether from false motives or true, Christ is preached. And because of this I rejoice. Yes, and I will continue to rejoice …" (Phil. 1:18).

A youth pastor at Shively Christian Church was very competitive with his neighbors at Shively Baptist Church. Once the pastor gave a Bible lesson from the thirteenth chapter of John about Jesus washing his disciples' feet. To help the young congregants become true disciples of Jesus, he divided them into small groups to go out and do community service. "I want you to be Jesus in the city for the next two hours," he said. "If Jesus were here, what would he do? Figure out how he would help people."

Two hours later the youth group re-gathered, and one group after another stood up and reported. The fifth group said that the elderly lady whom they had helped thought the young people belonged to Shively Baptist Church.

"Shively *Baptist*!" the pastor shouted. "I sure hope you set her straight and told her you were from Shively *Christian* Church."

"Why, no, we didn't," the kids said. "We didn't think it mattered."[2]

How insightful these kids were! Indeed, nothing matters as long as Christ is preached, as the apostle Paul said in Philippians 1:18: "The important thing is that in every way … Christ is preached." And whenever Christ is preached, we should rejoice.

Through Whatever Happens

While others might lose their faith when faced with adversity, faithful Christians will experience the power of the gospel in their sufferings. Eventually they will discover the great joy of the abundant life that Christ offers.

One girl named Rachel attended a public school that was a battlefield. Students were smuggling drugs into the school and joining gangs. No moral values existed. When she was a freshman, Rachel was diagnosed with leukemia. But she did not succumb to bitterness. Instead, she said, "I know that God can choose to heal me. But I'm going to bring as many people home with me into eternity as I can. I'm committed to making every day count for Jesus." Everyone was watching her to see if the illness would make her despondent. But she remained cheerful, showing others the peace God was offering her.

A few weeks after her sixteenth birthday, Rachel answered God's call to be with him in heaven. Hundreds of students rode a procession of school buses to her funeral. During the service, the pastor read a letter Rachel had written on her sixteenth birthday: "Dear Classmates: I told my parents that I was willing to die and go home into eternity if I could bring all of you with me. My Savior made a way for you to get to the other side …" After the letter was finished, almost all her friends and schoolmates offered themselves to Jesus Christ.[3]

Rachel lived as Paul proclaimed in Philippians 1:21: "To live is Christ and to die is gain." They both marched for Jesus. At some point, everyone considers his or her trials unbearable. But as long as our master Jesus Christ asks us to carry our own crosses and follow him, he will strengthen us and pull us through. We can do all things through Christ who gives us strength (Phil. 4:13).

My father rejected me when I was called into the pastorate. We were lunching on noodles at a restaurant when I told him, and he slapped the table and shouted, "After four years of college, you want to live in a temple your whole life!" He told me he was going to run an announcement in the local newspaper saying he was disowning me. To him, becoming a Christian meant I was dishonoring my father, my ancestors, and all of their traditions. But I knew I'd been called to advance the gospel. So I was willing to suffer as a result.

I took a train home to ask my mother for her support. When I arrived, my father had already left. He had taken off on his motorcycle and refused to see me or dine with me. For the first time since childhood, I knelt in front of my mother and cried. I told her I loved her but I loved Jesus, too. I believed if I answered his call, he would bless my family in return. Finally, in tears, my mother gave me her blessing, and asked me to leave before my father had a chance to return home and beat me. Off I ran to the train station. As I stood on the platform, my father suddenly showed up on his motorcycle, followed a few minutes later by my mother. I was scared to death. Then, just before my train was to depart, my father touched my shoulder and said, "Do well. Be a good young man. Your Jesus will take care of you." How I wished at that moment I could stay with my parents just one more night. With tears still running down my cheeks, I left them to follow the call of Jesus.

After I finished seminary in the states, my father's stance changed again. He told me over the phone that anything I might do in Taiwan would be better than pioneering a church here in San Jose in the heart of Silicon Valley. "What are you doing there in America? No money, no power! No nothing! You won't have anything as long as you remain a pastor."

Nonetheless, his actual visit here turned out much better than I had expected. Seeing me contributing in the community, helping the needy, and bringing living hope to the desperate, my father was touched. Somehow he was proud of me now. I remember he said, "As long as you enjoy your work. And actually, you're doing good by helping people." Then, later at the airport, he said, "Make an effort. Be diligent. You will have built a church as big as a company by the time I come to see you again."

Yet the second time he came, I was afraid to face him. By then my church, Living Hope, had crumbled. After returning from a missionary trip to Poland, I discovered most of my members had found other churches. All that remained of the congregation was one family. What could I do? How could I face my father? I was afraid he might think Christians were losers if his son, as a pastor, was suffering so much. But I realized I had no way of stopping him from visiting, so I determined to trust God more than ever. When my father came, all he saw was a storage room that was smaller than a two-car garage. Nonetheless, about one month later, he decided to give his heart to Jesus Christ. He offered a prayer confessing his sins to God, and Jesus Christ became his personal Savior. What had happened? He saw something he had never seen before—the joy I had in Christ, my boldness in restarting our church in San Jose immediately when church growth experts told me it would be impossible, and my fearlessness in the face of poverty. He saw that a storage room could be a sanctuary. He realized only one thing could have propelled his son forward in the face of such obstacles: Jesus Christ. He acknowledged Jesus must be real, and that his gospel must be real as well. I am not saying that he saw some kind of perfection in me. I am definitely imperfect. But what I've faced has truly served to advance the gospel.

If you have any encouragement from being united with Christ, if any comfort from his love, if any fellowship with the Spirit, if any tenderness and compassion, then make my joy complete by being like-minded, having the same love, being one in spirit and purpose. Do nothing out of selfish ambition or vain conceit, but in humility consider others better than yourselves. Each of you should look not only to your own interests, but also to the interests of others.

—Philippians 2:1–4

Chapter 2

TOGETHER WE HUMBLE OURSELVES

During my second year of seminary, I worked for the dean's secretary. I knew she had been a missionary prior to coming to our school, so one day, while I was walking her to her car to pick up some office files, I asked her what she considered the first qualification for serving the Lord.

"Humility," she said.

"How about the second qualification?" I asked.

The answer was the same.

"And the third?"

The answer was still the same. I understood that humility was crucial. But it wasn't until five years later that I really began taking this matter seriously.

A group of elderly ladies were chatting after an address by one of the pastors. Suddenly their conversation was disrupted by the shout of the pastor's young son, who had run up into the pulpit, seized the microphone, and shouted, "Look everybody, I'm the preacher. I'm in the pulpit!"

"His father preaches that way every Sunday," said one of the elderly women in disgust.

9

What a shame if my congregation had reason to speak that way of me. Be very careful, for many eyes are watching to see if you are humble or not.

How many times have we heard that we should have humility? The Bible warns us, "God opposes the proud but gives grace to the humble" (James 4:6). We will never taste grace in anything we do until we are humble—and that includes the mission of advancing the gospel. I want to continuously encourage all of us to advance the gospel, and as I do that humbly I am praying that I have come with grace. In chapter two of Philippians there are three types of grace, and I would like to share them with you: grace from others, grace for others, and the grace of God. With these, we can fulfill the mission entrusted to us.

Grace from Others

"But in humility consider others better than yourselves" (Phil. 2:3). That means we must always be able to find help in others. Even Paul, after his conversion on the Damascus Road, needed Barnabas to recommend him to other Christians as one of them. Without this endorsement Paul would have never been able to begin his ministry (Acts 11:25–26).

Anyone can help you whenever and wherever you are in need. So do not isolate yourself out of pride. You can't do everything. And when you admit that, you open yourself to others.

Recently, the light on my dashboard indicated it was time to add more coolant. I pulled into a gas station and immediately opened the cap. What happened? You probably know.

All of a sudden, I recalled what I had been taught—I should not open the cap while it is hot. But it was too late. What could I do? I went ahead and asked for help from the gentleman who spoke broken English and worked at the gas station. He was so sincere and he took care of my need as if it were his. He didn't even charge me.

Alex Haley, author of the sensational book *Roots,* has a picture in his office that reminds him of the importance of humility. It shows a turtle sitting on top of a fence. He hung that picture to remind him of a lesson he learned a long time ago: if you see a turtle on a fence

10

post, you know it got there with help from someone. Whenever Haley thinks about his success, the picture reminds him that he did not get there on his own. I also have this picture on my own wall.

People's need for help is greatest of all in times of danger. Ellie, a teenaged Jewish girl, tried to escape from a prison camp in Nazi Germany one night. She almost made it, but when she was halfway up the fence an S.S. guard spotted her. Raising his weapon, he commanded her to come down. She did so, with bleeding legs from the barbed wire fence. She began weeping, knowing all hope was gone. But, stunned, she heard the guard say, "Ellie? Is that you? It's not possible."

She looked into his face and realized it was Rolf, her best friend from middle school. "Oh, Rolf, go ahead and kill me. Please! I have no reason to live! I have lost all hope! Get it over with and let me die now. There's nothing to live for anyway."

"Ellie, you are so wrong," Rolf said. "There is everything to live for so long as you know *who* to live for. I'm going to let you go. I'll guard you until you climb the wall and get on the other side. But would you promise me one thing?"

"What is it, Rolf?" she said.

Rolf asked her to ask this one question until someone answered it for her: "Why does Jesus Christ make life worth living?"

As Ellie began to climb the fence, Rolf shouted, "He's the only reason to live. Promise me, Ellie! He's the only reason to live. Promise me that you'll ask until you get the answer." As she reached the other side, she heard gunshots. Looking back, she saw Rolf had been killed by the other S.S. guards. Ellie wondered who this Jesus Christ was, and why Rolf would give his life for her to know him. She kept her promise and learned why Jesus Christ makes life worth living. Later, Ellie came to America to testify as to who Jesus is, and what Jesus has done for us.[4] She knew that she had received grace.

Grace for Others

Philippians 2:4 reads, "Each of you should look not only to your own interests, but also to the interests of others." A humble person knows that whatever he or she owns comes from God.

We have rented a booth at World Journal Culture Center in San Jose. We call it Gospel Station, and we offer different community services, from free tutoring to lending Christian books. We have received so much from the Lord that we want to pass it on, and we want to do so quickly. We strongly believe we are a channel God can use to bless others. By giving to others, we demonstrate that God's grace is always sufficient for us. Whenever God touches our hearts and tells us to share, we must do so. The Bible is very clear on this: "Freely you have received, freely give" (Matt. 10:8). Praise the Lord!

Christians who are Christlike will certainly look to the interests of others, because that is exactly what Jesus would do. I am so proud of our church. On Sunday mornings, we see one of our beloved brothers rolling up his sleeves to clean the kitchen and bathroom, and to mop my humble office and our classroom. His wife and other sisters are busy with other tasks. Our pianist has served faithfully for almost two decades, bringing her children along, and now her husband has finally and joyfully joined us. We see other sisters and brothers visit and care for people and pray for one another during the weekdays.

Our youth care for our special needs children. They have served many lunches. They tell the world the message of God's grace, and they offer grace for others. By doing all of this and more, we are fulfilling Philippians 2:4, "Each of you should look not only to your own interests, but also to the interests of others."

When Paul the apostle was traveling and ministering in Macedonia, not one church supported him—except the church in Philippi. They offered him "full payment and even more." He blessed them, saying, "God will meet all your needs according to his glorious riches in Christ Jesus" (Phil. 4:18–19). We can learn from these early Christians. Keep up the good work. The more you give, the more you will receive. God remembers what you do with your own hands.

Are you familiar with the drawing called *The Praying Hands*? I have one in my office. Albrecht Durer painted it to honor his friend Franz Knigstein. When they were both struggling young artists, they agreed to draw lots and the loser would do manual work to support the two of them while the other learned art. Albrecht drew the winning lot and went off to the cities of Europe to pursue his studies.

After succeeding as a brilliant and talented artist, he went home to keep his promise. But Albrecht discovered how his friend had suffered to support him: Franz's fingers had stiffened due to manual labor, and he could no longer execute fine brushstrokes. All the same, Franz never stored bitterness in his heart. Instead he celebrated Albrecht's success. One day Albrecht found him kneeling, palms together, in solitary prayer. Albrecht heard him praying for the achievements of his beloved friend—Albrecht himself. Moved by this scene, Albrecht immediately sketched Franz's hands, and the drawing later became the masterpiece known as *The Praying Hands*.[5]

How beautiful these hands are! How pure Franz's heart was. Are you lifting up your hands to pray for others? To bless others? Are you willing to show grace for others as cheerfully as Albrecht and Franz did? If the Lord wants you to trust him by only looking to others' interests, are you willing to do so to bring people to Christ? That is what the Lord is looking for in you—a willingness to lay down your life, your interests, and your desires, all for the sake of the kingdom.

Paul had the same desire, as did his spiritual son Timothy. In his letter to the Philippians (2:21–22), we read: "For everyone looks out for his own interests, not those of Jesus Christ. But you know that Timothy has proved himself, because as a son with his father he has served with me in the work of the gospel." Let us join Paul and Timothy and keep up the conviction that God uses us to bless others and to show grace for others.

Grace of God

We can find the grace of God in Philippians 2:1–2, which says: "If you have any encouragement from being united with Christ, if any comfort from his love, if any fellowship with the Spirit, if any tenderness and compassion, then make my joy complete by being like-minded, having the same love, being one in spirit and purpose." The fourfold "if" in the verse emphasizes the conditions of receiving God's grace, proposing we must do something to receive what is promised to us. John F. Walvoord suggests translating "if" as "because." The author offers the following substitution: "It is *because* of the realities of God's grace, common to all Christians, that Christians should be of one mind."[6] We are reminded that God's grace is ready for us.

Paul knew better than anyone that asking Christians to be humble and to look to the interests of others is not easy. Instead, the apostle pointed us to the resource: Christ. In Christ, we have encouragement, because we are united with him. In Christ, we have comfort, because of his everlasting love. In Christ, we enjoy sweet fellowship with the Spirit. In Christ, we will taste tenderness and compassion. God's grace is absolutely sufficient! Our work is to believe we are united with Christ. And the love of Christ will compel us to enjoy God's grace more.

From now on, let us do nothing out of selfish ambition or vain conceit, but in humility consider others better than ourselves. Each of us should look not only to our own interests, but also to the interests of others. We have the resource to help us be humble. It is all in Christ. It is all in God's grace. In his grace, we freely receive grace from others.

Ralph Shing-Gwai Chan was a Hong Kong movie star. He proposed marriage to Alice, a TV producer, and she agreed to his proposal on one condition—that he would vow to maintain a God-glorified marriage. Without hesitation, Ralph agreed. While they were making their wedding preparations, however, Ralph found himself easily exhausted. Since he was still very young, the couple did not think much about it. When Ralph's fatigue persisted, shocking news soon followed: Ralph had cancer of the nasal cavity. Her pastor comforted Alice and told her that God has a will of his own. Nevertheless, Ralph, once a handsome movie star, ended up with a twisted face after radiation therapy. He could hardly drink water and his body smelled. Because Ralph's face was so disfigured, people no longer recognized him as Ralph Chan the movie star. But he asked his beautiful wife Alice to go out and testify to the love of Christ.

Upon witnessing their struggles, Ralph's cousin accepted Jesus as his personal Savior, saying, "I have heard people talk about Jesus hundreds of times. Now, I know that Ralph's Jesus is real." As they gave their testimony, Alice and Ralph made Psalm 46 their gospel song:

God is our refuge and strength, an ever-present help in trouble.
Therefore we will not fear, though the earth gives way
And the mountains fall into the heart of the sea,
Though its waters roar and foam and the mountains quake
with their surging.

Come, enjoy God's grace, humbly receiving blessing and humbly giving it away. Together, we will introduce Ralph's Jesus to thousands upon thousands of people.

Paul, an apostle of Christ Jesus by the will of God, according to the promise of life that is in Christ Jesus, To Timothy, my dear son: Grace, mercy and peace from God the Father and Christ Jesus our Lord.

—2 Timothy 1:1–2

Chapter 3

TOGETHER WE BEAR
THE TORCH

On March 31, 2008, after months of waiting, the Olympic torch was flown into Beijing and met by General Secretary Hu Jintao. Starting from Beijing, the torch would begin a round-the-world tour. This torch relay was the longest in Olympic history, covering 85,000 miles across six continents in 130 days. We were desperate to watch it. Some of us even wanted to participate. I believe if the apostle Paul had still been alive, he would have used this opportunity to summon us to run another type of torch relay, not one for the Olympics, but for the gospel of Christ.

Bearing the Gospel Torch

In his day, the apostle Paul held the torch for the gospel and ran the relay. When he knew his final hours had come and sensed the urgency of his situation, he wanted to pass the torch to Timothy, and then, through Timothy, to others. He wanted to see us, generation after generation, proudly bearing it and running the relay until one day we are met by the King of kings, Christ Jesus! In the Olympics, only a few select people can bear the torch, but all Christians are called to bear and pass on the gospel torch.

The road ahead is not an easy one for those who are willing to bear the torch for the gospel of Christ. That is why, in the beginning of his letters to Timothy, Paul calls him his spiritual son. Not only does Paul remind Timothy to be unashamed of the gospel, he also invites him to suffer boldly for it. Throughout the letter, written when he was about to depart this world, Paul stands tall, showing that we should be proud of the good news.

Now, if Paul were with us today, he would tell us to take pride in bearing the gospel torch, pride no less than we would take in bearing the Olympic torch. And this is the message I want to share.

Let's dive into the first two verses of 2 Timothy: "Paul, an apostle of Christ Jesus by the will of God, according to the promise of life that is in Christ Jesus, to Timothy, my dear son: Grace, mercy, and peace from God the Father and Christ Jesus our Lord." The introduction of the letter teaches us that we should tell the world of the gospel, to fan into flame the gift of God within us. Thus, we are living according to the promise of life in Christ Jesus. The apostle Paul wished Timothy to experience grace, mercy, and peace from God the Father and Christ Jesus our Lord. And as bearers of the gospel torch, we too are telling the world that, in Christ, we will find grace, mercy, and peace.

Sensing God's Mercy

Let's start with mercy. Interestingly, of Paul's many letters, only in the last ones to Timothy do we find the word *mercy* in the greeting. Why is that? The second letter to Timothy was Paul's final epistle and it contains his last known words to his spiritual son right before his death. Some call this letter his last will to Timothy, and through him, to us. I believe that after many years of serving the Lord, Paul realized that if God does not show us mercy first, we are all under his wrath. We all deserve to be punished because of our sins, but the Lord spares us from his justice. This is mercy. Though Paul had greeted the church only with "grace" and "peace" in his many previous letters, in the end he hoped for God's compassion.

In this letter, Paul describes his past to show God's clemency:

> Even though I was once a blasphemer and a persecutor and a violent man, I was shown mercy … Here is a trustworthy saying that deserves full acceptance: Christ Jesus came into the world to save sinners—of whom I am the worst. But for that very reason I was shown mercy so that in me, the worst of sinners, Christ Jesus might display his unlimited patience as an example for those who would believe on him and receive eternal life.
>
> —1 Timothy 1:13, 15–16

Paul felt like the worst of sinners. That was exactly how I felt when I first encountered the love of Jesus Christ, my personal Savior. When I was a young student, I persecuted Christians out of ignorance. When my Christian classmate told me we could find joy in Christ, I thought he was a hypocrite because he smiled all the time. How could he be so happy? I didn't understand how he could say that in God we can always rejoice. I was in middle school then, and my family was in serious debt. My father gambled all the time, so my mother and I needed to work whenever we could.

As I recall, my attitude toward Christians grew even worse in my first year of high school. On two occasions when I saw people distributing Bibles in front of the school gate, I grabbed all I could, took them home, and burned them in a big garbage can. As I watched the Bibles bursting into flame, I felt excited and proud. I thought I was doing humankind a great favor by preventing false teachings from spreading and contaminating innocent minds.

Then came the day that changed me completely. The Christian classmate invited me to his high school fellowship. I thought I would show off my courage by accepting the invitation. Upon learning that this was my first time in church, the speaker changed his entire message and made it very simple. He talked about how Jesus Christ died for our sins. Hearing his message, my eyes filled with tears. When the speaker asked me whether I would like to accept Jesus Christ as my personal Savior, I nodded. After saying a prayer, I sensed—for the first time in my life—that I was loved, that I was forgiven. The speaker took me home on his motorcycle. As we rode by the ocean along a beautiful coastline, I heard the waves splash back and forth, welcoming me. I could smell cool salt as the wind blew over my face. When sunset cast its golden light over me, I felt sprinkled with joy. For the first time I appreciated the beauty of my city, Hualien. Everything looked fresh and blessed by God's love.

Have you ever sensed that God's mercy is boundless and deep? Come, let us bear the gospel torch and tell people of God's charity. Let us tell them that the Lord will not keep a ledger of sins, so that we are all able to stand! (Ps. 130:3–4). Let us bear the torch and tell others that God does not store up anger but delights in showing his mercy. He will again have compassion on us. He will trample our sins underfoot and hurl all our iniquities into the depths of the sea (Mic. 7:18–19). I strongly believe that this is what the apostle Paul experienced. He sensed the ocean of God's mercy.

God's Amazing Grace

We speak not only of God's mercy, but also of God's amazing *grace*. What amazing grace! Whoever believes in Christ will receive eternal life! By God's grace we are saved. And in 2 Timothy, we are shown another kind of grace: God's grace gives us blessed assurance. Paul says, "Yet I am not ashamed, because I know whom I have believed, and am convinced that he is able to guard what I have entrusted to him for that day" (2 Tim. 1:12). Think about Paul, for here he seems here to stand very tall. While people outside were wondering whether he suffered in prison, he had blessed assurance that God would feed and shelter him.

In Christ we have mercy and grace. What is grace? It is God giving us divine assistance when we don't deserve it. What is mercy? That God does not give us what we do deserve. There is a world of difference. The good we don't deserve, God gives us anyway. This is grace. The bad that is the consequences of our own actions, which we *do* deserve, God does not give us. This is mercy.

We can't give ourselves grace. We need someone else to give it to us. In Christ, we have amazing grace! In Christ, God is willing to give us grace—the grace that rescues us from sin and leads us to salvation, and the grace that embraces us. We can entrust everything to him, because he will guard us until the end. We can testify to people as Paul did. What the Lord said to Paul, he is saying to us today in 2 Corinthians 12:9–10:

> My grace is sufficient for you, for my power is made perfect in weakness. Therefore I will boast all the more gladly about my weaknesses, so that Christ's power may rest on me. That is why, for Christ's sake, I delight in weaknesses, in insults, in hardships, in persecutions, in difficulties. For when I am weak, then I am strong.

In Corinth one night, the Lord spoke to Paul in a vision: "Do not be afraid; keep on speaking, do not be silent. For I am with you, and no one is going to attack and harm you, because I have many people in this city" (Acts 18:9–11). Therefore, Paul stayed for over a year, teaching the Corinthians the Word of God. Paul had much support from faithful friends, and their encouragement energized him and helped him establish the church in Corinth.

The Lord knows exactly what we need, when we need it. He provides help for us so long as we bear the gospel torch. Even if we have no friends to support us, God is always waiting to aid us as long as we turn to him.

I had a tough time during my first few years of pioneering a church in San Jose, California. At Living Hope Church, we were in a constant financial struggle. Even worse, I didn't know how to deal with some of the problems. For example, three years had passed before I finally realized I had been deeply hurt by someone in my community. I had convinced myself that there was no problem. But at a certain point, I realized these issues had in fact grown from a minor conflict into outright hatred. For the first time in my life, I knew what it meant to be truly wounded. This experience was unnerving and incredibly upsetting, so much so that I initially forgot to turn to Christ. The problem simmered, unresolved. Eventually, it consumed me completely, both physically and emotionally.

At five one morning, I woke with severe chest pains, as if a needle had been stuck into my heart. I was sharing a small bedroom with my wife and two children, since my parents-in-law were sleeping in the master bedroom. Afraid of waking my family, I stuffed the comforter into my mouth and hurried to my study, where I hid myself in my prayer closet. Crying muffled tears, I was too emotionally weak to call "Lord," or "Jesus," or as I usually called out, "heavenly Father." I felt stranded in a vast emptiness. All I could say was, "What can I do? What can I do?" I knew I had to come before the Lord. I knew he was my all in all. I knew that he understood I was too exhausted to call him "Lord." I just came to him, crying out as to my best friend, "What can I do? What can I do?" Then I heard a soft voice. I knew it was from the Lord. The voice urged me to go downstairs for my daily devotion.

It had been a while since I had immersed myself in a good devotion. Humbly, I opened the weekly church bulletin and turned to the devotional schedule. I flipped open Psalm 55 and was shocked to find that I was experiencing exactly what had happened to the psalmist. As he too had been betrayed by his friend, the psalmist's every word spoke to my situation. Then came the Bible verse that made me burst into tears again, the *rhema*, God's word to me—"Cast your cares on the LORD and he will sustain you; he will never let the righteous fall" (Ps. 55:22). I knew it! These were the words that came to me from the mouth of God. They were like a spring shower, and I was instantly refreshed.

Come! "Taste and see that the LORD is good; blessed is the man who takes refuge in him … The lions may grow weak and hungry, but those who seek the LORD lack no good thing" (Ps. 34:8–10). This is what the torchbearers of the gospel can tell the world. While serving the Lord and reaching out to people for the sake of Christ, we must deal with rudeness or even conflict, and we need support. We are telling people that the grace of the Lord will be shown to all of us, as Paul said at the end of his two letters to Timothy. We do not deserve it, but God wants to give it to us anyway; that is why it is called grace. And my God will meet all your needs according to his glorious riches in Christ Jesus (Phil. 4:19).

In his letters, the apostle Paul talks about how God, by his grace and loving kindness, sent him a dear friend. When people were deserting

Paul because he was imprisoned in Ephesus, God sent Onesiphorus and all his family to search everywhere until he found him and could reassure him in person (2 Tim. 1:16–17). Onesiphorus' friendship comforted and refreshed Paul in his time of need. And so Paul prayed for his family to receive special kindness.

Just as only one family stood with Paul, only one family stood with me after my church, Living Hope, finally crumbled. From raising funds twenty-five cents at a time at garage sales to walking the streets to pass out church information, the children of this family joined their parents to lift our church from the dead. When I had no students to teach, the family insisted I hold a tiny Sunday school and teach their kids along with my own. On sunny days, we met in the park; on rainy days we moved to El Pollo Loco™, a Mexican restaurant. I remember telling the parents, "I can't give your children anything. I know, however, one day, I will take your children to give people something." That something was God's grace. By his providing me with the family, I can say God is the God who comforts us. He is "the God and Father of our Lord Jesus Christ, the Father of compassion and the God of all comfort" (2 Cor. 1:3).

I would like to thank God for all of those who have been with me building up the church for God's glory. Surrounded by such stalwarts of the faith, I have no fear of spreading the gospel. Even with my stuttering problem, I have courage to tell about Jesus' love. Because of you, I can always sleep soundly. Praise the Lord. Here and now and whenever I am preaching I have no fear and no hesitation. This is because of God's special grace: that those who are God's gifts to me are with me.

Finding Peace in Christ

At this point, Paul wishes for Timothy to enjoy not only mercy and grace, but also the *peace* he will find in Christ. Peace is a fantastic gift! When we are reconciled with God, we are guaranteed peace with him. Praise the Lord! There is no peace on earth among humankind, but through the finished work of Christ we are promised not only peace with God but also the peace of God as we walk in his grace each day. And from Paul's teaching in the fourth chapter of Philippians, we know how to experience this peace: through prayer.

> Rejoice in the Lord always. I will say it again: Rejoice! Let your gentleness be evident to all. The Lord is near. Do not be anxious about anything, but in everything, by prayer and petition, with thanksgiving, present your requests to God. And the peace of God, which transcends all understanding, will guard your hearts and your minds in Christ Jesus.
>
> —Philippians 4:4–7

Pray to God and enjoy an immense sense of peace. That wisdom was Paul's secret. Otherwise, he could not have survived his many ordeals. From 2 Corinthians chapter eleven we know that he had been imprisoned many times, flogged severely, and often exposed to death. Five times he received the "forty lashes minus one" from the Jews. But none of these hardships could stop him from enjoying the peace of God. He knew he was safe so long as he was willing to be embraced by Christ Jesus.

Take a look at what he wanted to do before his departure from this life: "I am already being poured out like a drink offering, and the time has come for my departure" (2 Tim. 4:6). He tells Timothy: "Get Mark and bring him with you, because he is helpful to me in my ministry ... When you come, bring the cloak that I left with Carpus at Troas, and my scrolls, especially the parchments" (2 Tim. 4:11, 13). He is not concerned about death. Instead, he is focusing on doing God's work, taking care of his health, and reading some good books. How peaceful! How powerful! Only a man of prayer can live such a peaceful life, for he is with Christ all the time! We are torchbearers of the gospel, and we can experience the same peace.

When my mother was in the final stage of her terminal stomach cancer, I thought God would heal her. Before leaving my second year of seminary to fly to her in Taiwan, I told everyone to expect a miracle. Yet three hours after I arrived at my brother's home, my mother passed away. I prayed for God to raise her from the dead. But God did not do what I asked. My father held a traditional Chinese funeral for her, but my cries were louder than the trumpets in the funeral band. At the end,

I tapped my mother's casket and whispered, "My God, my God, why have you forsaken me?"

After the funeral, I had to rush back home to Tulsa since my wife Susan was about to give birth. This was the most difficult journey I had ever faced. I knew when the plane landed I would have to face people who had heard me say God would raise my mother from the dead. I kept asking God why. Why me? When I had prayed for others, they were healed, but when I prayed for my own mother, she was not. Why? God did not say a word. Then, as I wiped some vapor from the window of the plane, a gentle voice whispered to me, "Do you love me more than these?"

Tears came. "Yes, Lord, I am willing to love you."

What a divine encounter. Yes, I did love Jesus "more than these"— more than being right, more than having my foolish predictions come true. I knew that God had humbled me in order to make me wise, and I welcomed the humiliation, knowing that Jesus would always see me through. The Lord did not answer my questions but asked me his own question instead, and after I answered my doubts disappeared and my sorrows left completely. I experienced the peace of God. The peace of God is not the absence of life's storms, but the presence of Christ in the storms. In Christ I can enjoy peace all the time.

To all, *grace, mercy,* and *peace* from God the Father and Christ Jesus our Lord. By holding the flame high and keeping it burning, we are telling the world that in God and through Christ we will always have grace, mercy, and peace. Let us run together with the torch of the gospel.

On the third day a wedding took place at Cana in Galilee. Jesus' mother was there, and Jesus and his disciples had also been invited to the wedding. When the wine was gone, Jesus' mother said to him, "They have no more wine." "Dear woman, why do you involve me?" Jesus replied, "My time has not yet come." His mother said to the servants, "Do whatever he tells you." Nearby stood six stone water jars, the kind used by the Jews for ceremonial washing, each holding from twenty to thirty gallons. Jesus said to the servants, "Fill the jars with water"; so they filled them to the brim. Then he told them, "Now draw some out and take it to the master of the banquet." They did so, and the master of the banquet tasted the water that had been turned into wine. He did not realize where it had come from, though the servants who had drawn the water knew. Then he called the bridegroom aside and said, "Everyone brings out the choice wine first and then the cheaper wine after the guests have had too much to drink; but you have saved the best till now." This, the first of his miraculous signs, Jesus performed in Cana of Galilee. He thus revealed his glory, and his disciples put their faith in him.

—John 2:1–11

Chapter 4

TOGETHER WE ENJOY ABUNDANT LIFE IN CHRIST

Who is Nick Vujicic? He was born without arms and legs. But watch Nick swim. Watch him golf. Watch one high school girl hugging him with tears rolling down her face. Look at how he enjoys everything. Nick's every moment inspires. Thousands upon thousands of people have been touched by his life. Although he has no limbs, he seems to fly. What is the secret of his success? "No matter who you are, no matter what you're going through, God knows it," he says. "He is with you. He is going to pull you through." Nick continues spreading the Word of God through a program of 1,600 speaking appearances in twelve nations entitled "Attitude is Altitude."[7] Jesus Christ brought him a joyful life, and by exemplifying a life filled with joy, Nick introduces his Savior to all of us.

The gospel hymn "In Christ Alone" says it so well:

> "In Christ alone my hope is found.
> He is my light, my strength, my song;
> This cornerstone, this solid ground,
> Firm through the fiercest drought and storm.
> What heights of love, what depths of peace,
> When fears are stilled, when strivings cease!
> My comforter, my all in all—Here in the love of Christ I stand."[8]

27

Through the strength of Christ alone, Nick exudes joy in even the smallest of tasks. Through the strength of Christ alone, Nick wakes up, brushes his teeth, combs his hair, and rides his motorcycle. Through Christ alone, Nick shows us how he has turned his trials into triumphs. And now, traveling around the world, Nick tells us all that in Christ Jesus we can accomplish anything!

Whenever a person feels overwhelmed, faith in God will bring him through the crisis to happiness. Life without limbs was a terrible burden for Nick and gave him little chance for joy. He even thought of committing suicide as young as age eight. Yet by coming to Jesus in faith and trust, Nick lives an extraordinarily vital and meaningful life. Come, taste the abundant life in Christ Jesus. Everything you need for peace and joy, you can find in Jesus Christ.

In antiquity, guests at a wedding banquet expected several days of fine food and wine. If the wine ran out, the host family was disgraced. We can imagine how the hosts of the wedding at Cana must have worried about the feelings of the wedding couple, the pleasure of the guests, and the pride of the family hosting the celebration. But imagine how relieved and joyful the hosts must have felt when they realized that not only was there plenty of wine, but thanks to Jesus, the best wine had actually been saved for last.

What matters to us matters to Jesus. Throughout John's gospel the Lord intervenes in people's lives to be the generous giver of all good things: "Jesus did many other miraculous signs in the presence of his disciples, which are not recorded in this book. But these are written that you may believe that Jesus is the Christ, the Son of God, and that by believing you may have life in his name" (John 20:30–31).

When Feeling Desperate

Many people across America watch the television series *Desperate Housewives*. It is popular because it relates to the feelings that ordinary folks like you and I have. Do you sometimes feel you are in a desperate situation with only despair and no hope? Are you a desperate husband? A desperate student? A desperate worker? A desperate lover? A desperate parent? The more you think about your insurmountable problems, the more desperate you become. But we need to have faith in Christ Jesus, a faith that allows us to see his glory manifested in joyfully abundant life. After bearing witness to the miracle of water turning into wine, John writes, "He thus revealed his glory, and his disciples put their faith in him" (John 2:11).

Indeed, with God, all things are possible even in the face of tragedy. On December 10, 2008, an F/A-18D plane crashed into the home of Korean immigrant Dong Yun Yoon of San Diego, killing his wife, two daughters, and mother-in-law. Yet he had no hard feelings toward the military pilot of the jet, who ejected from the plane just before it crashed. He even called him an American treasure for his service to his country, saying, "I believe my wife and two babies and mother-in-law are in heaven with God."[9] Dong Yun Yoon has truly testified to the power of faith.

How desperate are you in your current situation? Are you able to proclaim what Robert Reed proclaims? Despite crippled hands and feet due to cerebral palsy, he has achieved success as a college professor and missionary to Portugal. He has overcome unbelievable obstacles that would have crushed an ordinary spirit. Though his speech drags, he exclaims, holding his bent hand up in the air, "I have everything I need for joy!"[10]

Don't you also wish your life were held together by joy? Are you *really* convinced that Jesus is the One to whom you can appeal? Do you really, firmly believe that in the midst of your anxiety, Jesus is still your Lord? He is not just the Lord of Sunday morning worship services. You have to believe that he is your Lord in everyday life.

How I Found Hope in Christ

Let me tell you about my darkest hours of Christian service. My church, Living Hope, was closing. What could I do? Where should I go? I considered returning to my temporary ministry in Europe; however, I knew that the Lord wanted me to stay in San Jose and restart my church. Every time I ran into people from my previous church, I felt I was letting them down. Without a church or an income, I had run out of wine at my wedding banquet.

One evening, I knelt down and sobbed to my dear Lord. "Please take care of those I cherish. I lift up my family into your hands. If you want me to die here because I have failed, I am willing. One thing I ask you, Lord: let me die with dignity. My death is in your hands. Lord, help me. Lord, restore me. Lord, anoint me with oil of joy. Lord, it is you who wants to restart my church. Lord, here I am. I am coming to you." After my prayer, I fell into a deep sleep.

When I woke, I found myself filled with renewed certainty. A deep peace flowed through me. God had filled me with the knowledge that, by remaining in the San Jose area, I was fulfilling his will. Praise the Lord! I instantly thought of the words in Psalm 30:4–5: "Sing to the LORD, you saints of his; praise his holy name. For his anger lasts only a moment, but his favor lasts a lifetime; weeping may remain for a night, but rejoicing comes in the morning." This experience taught me to listen very carefully to what Jesus says in John 16:24: "Until now you have not asked for anything in my name. Ask and you will receive, and your joy will be complete."

In Christ alone do you have everything promised in the Bible. Keep on believing; you will eventually see God's glory. "Rejoice in God always. I say it again: Rejoice! Do not be anxious about anything, but in everything, by prayer and petition, with thanksgiving, present your requests to God" (Phil. 4:4, 6). Prayer should not be the last resort. It should be the first because it is the most important step to cope with your problems. Be like Mary who knew to come to Jesus Christ.

At the wedding in Cana, Mary said to the servants, "Do whatever he tells you," and so too should we encourage each other by faith. In coming to Jesus for help, we must trust him completely. Even if his request is strange, the Lord works in ways we cannot see. Whatever the Lord wants us to do, we must do it!

Do not miss one day of living in God's promise. You don't have to wait for your life to fall apart to come to Jesus. Come to him while you still have wine—while you are still feeling good about yourself. Go to Jesus day after day. Know his voice. Depend upon him, for he is trustworthy.

While a large crowd was gathering and people were coming to Jesus from town after town, he told this parable: "A farmer went out to sow his seed. As he was scattering the seed, some fell along the path; it was trampled on, and the birds of the air ate it up. Some fell on rock, and when it came up, the plants withered because they had no moisture. Other seed fell among thorns, which grew up with it and choked the plants. Still other seed fell on good soil. It came up and yielded a crop, a hundred times more than was sown." When he said this, he called out, "He who has ears to hear, let him hear."

"This is the meaning of the parable: The seed is the word of God. Those along the path are the ones who hear, and then the devil comes and takes away the word from their hearts, so that they may not believe and be saved. Those on the rock are the ones who receive the word with joy when they hear it, but they have no root. They believe for a while, but in the time of testing they fall away. The seed that fell among thorns stands for those who hear, but as they go on their way they are choked by life's worries, riches and pleasures, and they do not mature. But the seed on good soil stands for those with a noble and good heart, who hear the word, retain it, and by persevering produce a crop."

—Luke 8:4–8, 11–15

Chapter 5

TOGETHER WE GROW IN FAITH

"Son, I want you to grow up healthier and stronger than me." I saw these words on a billboard ad for life insurance when I was a teenager. Since then, I have kept these sentiments in my heart, and I share them with you now to help you grow healthier and stronger in your faith in Jesus Christ—faith that is even stronger than mine.

To help us do this, let's look at Luke 8:4–16. Here, Jesus tells a parable to show us what can hinder our spiritual growth. As seeds must be planted in the soil to produce a crop, so the Word must be planted in our hearts for us to grow spiritually.

What can hinder our spiritual growth? Where do the problems lie? In the parable, what could possibly hinder plant growth? Is the problem the seed or the sower? Neither. Only with the right kind of soil will the seed yield a fruitful harvest. In the same way, we need the right humility, the right discernment, and the right responsiveness toward God's Word in order to grow healthier and stronger in our faith.

The Lord wants us to bear fruit—fruit that will increase our faith thirtyfold, sixtyfold, or even a hundredfold. How does that happen? Let's examine the parable of the sower and find out.

Open Your Heart to God

When the seeds of the Word of God tumble onto a path rather than into fertile soil, Jesus shows us they represent a person who hears the Word but allows the Devil to snatch his seeds away. A path is a form of dried-out earth sealed from change. As dried-out earth has no room for seeds, so the hard heart has no room for the Word of God. What should we do then? As we must find the right place to nurture seeds, our hearts must be fertile and ready to receive the Bible's teaching.

We must overturn our stubbornness! No matter how perfect we think we are, in some areas of our lives, our hearts are crusted over and inflexible. Whether this manifests as intolerance or selfishness, we must acknowledge and overcome our flaws.

Sometimes, we are hard-hearted like Pharaoh. When Moses confronted him with God's Word, Pharaoh knew he should let the Israelites go. Yet he refused ten times, prompting more devastating plagues each time he relented and then changed his mind. Not until all the firstborn were killed did Pharaoh realize God's command was imperative. Like Pharaoh, we sometimes don't listen. We must be "all ears" to what the Lord is saying: "He who has ears to hear, let him hear."

Hear carefully what the Lord says to you through sermons and fellowship with other Christians. Since the Bible says "Do not let the sun go down while you are still angry," dig up your anger (Eph. 4:26). Plow up your stubbornness. Remember that the best anger management available is that of going to Jesus. Trust he will give you peace. Just listen and do what he says. Open your heart wide, and allow the authority of the Word to be absolute in your life.

Focus on God's Words

We will become like shallow and rocky soil if we have no conviction in God's authority. There the seed sprouts quickly, but when the sun rises, the plants are scorched, and they wither because they have no roots. The shallow soil represents a shallow heart. People with shallow hearts receive the Word with joy when they first hear it, but have no foundation. They wish to follow Christ, but in times of testing, they fall away. Didn't Peter fail to recognize Jesus when asked whether or not he belonged to Jesus' group? Peter only had conditional conviction. Fearing to face the same doom as Jesus, the apostle denied him three times. He didn't obey God's Word completely because he wasn't fully committed at that moment in his life.

Watch out! Too many people taste God's power because of temporary devotion, but this is not true conversion. God may test us at any time to see if we have really turned to him or not. While authentic faith can impassion, it also requires fortitude. Unless you receive God's Word with conviction, your heart will remain shallow and superficial.

How do we find this conviction? Meditate! This is what the Lord asked of Joshua before he entered the Promised Land: "Do not let this Book of the Law depart from your mouth; meditate on it day and night, so that you may be careful to do everything written in it. Then you will be prosperous and successful" (Josh. 1:8). Joshua was told to meditate on God's Word day and night. Generation after generation, this is what the Lord wants his people to do.

Every serious Christian needs to make an effort to meditate on God's Word. In my case, I use a system I call "four plus three." Interestingly, such a system appears in Psalm 119 as well: "Seven times a day I praise you for your righteous laws" (Ps. 119:164). The "four plus three" procedure is a constant diet of Scripture throughout the day. Spend a few minutes meditating when you wake up and just before going to bed. Meditate before each of your three meals. Take another couple of minutes between breakfast and lunch and another couple between lunch and dinner. Try it for six weeks. Once you are in the habit, you can establish any consistent course of meditation that fits your schedule better.

To root God's Word in our heart, we have to come to it as often as possible. Consider the difference between a strong and a weak cup of tea. The same ingredients—water and tea—are used for both. The longer the steeping process, however, the stronger the drink. In the same way, the length of time we spend in God's Word determines how deeply we incorporate it into our lives and how deeply it permeates our hearts. Like the tea, the longer we are in Scripture the stronger we become.

Worldly Thorns

As an earnest believer, you already desire conviction from God's Word. But you may find it difficult to achieve. Why? It is because there is a wild force constantly seeking to tear us away. In his parable, Jesus describes this force as thorns choking a third type of soil. When seeds are sown on this soil and then watered, the thorns also grow, choking the plant before it can produce fruit.

The thorns represent the worries of this life, the deceitfulness of wealth, and the love of the world. All these things seek to destroy us and tempt our hearts away from spiritual concerns. People with divided hearts believe in the Bible, but its words do not have pride of place in their lives. They hear and believe in God's Word and want to do his will, but they are carried away by the word of the world.

The deceitfulness of wealth draws them with the promise of great things. They buy things they do not need to impress people they do not like with money they do not have. This is a divided heart—like the heart of the girl to whom a young man once proposed. He said, "Darling, I want you to know that I love you more than anything else in the world. I want you to marry me. I'm not rich. I don't have a helicopter or a TV show like Donald Trump, but I do love you with all my heart."

She thought for a minute and then replied, "I love you with all my heart too, but tell me more about Donald Trump."

A heart that is overcome with love for riches and possessions is not a believing heart. Those with such hearts are strangled by their love for this world; it's as if they say, "I love you with all my heart, God, but tell me what the world can do for me." You cannot serve two masters. Jesus said that "no one can serve two masters. Either he will hate the one and love the other, or he will be devoted to the one and despise the other. You cannot serve both God and Money" (Matt. 6:24). Worldly concerns will choke your faith if you try serving two masters, and you will bear no fruit.

Grow in Your Love of God

Moses encouraged the Israelites to love the Lord with all their heart, with all their soul, and with all their strength (Deut. 6:4–5). When we do the same we can resist temptation. One of the best practical ways to do this is to set aside Sunday as the Lord's Day. Make this the day you come to worship the Almighty God, take part in holy communion, study the Word, join in fellowship with other believers, silently reflect on your deeds before the Lord, and examine any hidden sins you may have. Get rid of everything hindering your spiritual growth.

Satan will not let you go easily. To find bugs, a woodpecker finds the right tree and begins to drill a hole. If it doesn't find them, it moves over and drills more holes until it succeeds. This is how Satan works. He will try as many temptations and distractions as possible to find a soft spot in us that he can use to his advantage.[11]

As E. Schuyler English comments:

> Temptation is to see the tempter standing outside the back door of your heart. Sin is to unlock that door so that he may have his desire. Victory is to open wide the front door of your heart, inviting the Savior to enter and give you strength to bar tight the back door.[12]

Humbly, I would like to invite you to open wide the front door of your heart.

Years ago, I picked up a notepad from a bank that had pictures on both the front and back covers. On the front, a grandpa is planting a little seedling with his grandson, who is wearing his hat backwards. They are watering the plant together under a beautiful blue sky with dreamy white clouds floating above. On the back of the notepad, the grandpa and grandson are sitting on a bench, smiling at the towering tree they have planted together. And the grandson, still wearing his hat backwards, is embracing his grandpa. We do not need to plant a lot of seeds to reap a big harvest. The seeds we plant only need good soil.

In what particular areas of your life would you like to see a harvest? Would you like to be a better husband? A better employee? A better witness for Christ? Whatever area of your life needs to be redeemed, start small. Plant the seed with the right heart and God will do the rest.

Therefore, since we are surrounded by such a great cloud of witnesses, let us throw off everything that hinders and the sin that so easily entangles, and let us run with perseverance the race marked out for us. Let us fix our eyes on Jesus, the author and perfecter of our faith, who for the joy set before him endured the cross, scorning its shame, and sat down at the right hand of the throne of God. Consider him who endured such opposition from sinful men, so that you will not grow weary and lose heart.

—Hebrews 12:1–3

Chapter 6

TOGETHER WE RUN!

Bang! We set off running on the fine sand, a scuffed track stretching out before us. Our shoes are tied tight. Surrounding us in an immense arena are the cheering spectators: our relatives, friends, schoolteachers, and strangers. A cloudless sky arcs above us in a vast dome. Our teammates, the heroes such as Abraham, Noah, Moses, and Elijah, hand us their batons and then line up behind us, encouraging us. They are all in the Hall of Fame—I mean the Hall of Faith. Now they wave and shout, "Keep on running. You can overcome the challenge. No matter how tough your life may seem, do not give up. Hang on a little longer, for God will make a way for you."

To help us finish the race, God gives us guidelines in Hebrews 12:1–3. All we have to do is prepare and run! We must discard everything that hinders us to run the race with perseverance. Doubts and weakness may hinder our determination, but we run in faith anyway. By faith, Abraham made a great nation. By faith, Moses brought his people out of Egypt. And like them, if we believe, we will win.

Stick with Your Race

In the movie *Chariots of Fire*, young champion sprinter Harold Abrahams suffered his first-ever defeat. After the race, he sat alone, pouting in the bleachers. When his girlfriend tried to encourage him, he said, "If I can't win, I won't run!"

"If you don't run, you can't win," she said.[13]

Abrahams went on to win the 1924 Olympic Gold Medal in the hundred-meter dash.

If we run, we will win. And so the author of Hebrews encourages believers to take on life's race with perseverance. Why? Because life is a distance race; with staying power we will complete it, and we will win! Go out and watch a stonecutter hammering away at a rock. He might hit the rock a hundred times without so much as a crack showing. Then, suddenly, on the hundred-and-first blow, the rock splits. Was it the last blow that split the rock? Of course not. That final blow would have accomplished nothing had it not been for the hundred prior blows.

Every day, Columbus wrote the following words in the log of the Santa Maria: "This day we sailed on!"[14] He believed he would find his destination, and finally he did. With faith, start your spiritual journal today. Log God's constancy to you and you will marvel at what you discover. Remember, God remains steadfast even when you falter.

The former model Christine Kent's best feature had always been her legs. Now, she says they feel like gelatin. Kent, forty-five, was paralyzed after a man shot her in the back three years ago and ran her over with his SUV. Still, without use of her legs, Kent found strength in her arms. She started hand cycling and later she completed the Fort Lauderdale A1A Marathon.

Although she lives in excruciating pain, the tragedy strengthened her Christian faith and altruism. From her wheelchair Kent leans down to help a blind woman pull weeds. She cooks dinner for a jobless neighbor. To those who are suffering she gives a simple piece of advice: "You can pick [yourself] up and become a better person for it."[15]

Travel Light

Having encouraged you to run with perseverance, I can now offer a second piece of guidance: Throw off everything that hinders you and the sins that so easily entangle you. In races, athletes shed all excess weight and carry nothing with them, and athletes of the Christian faith should do likewise. We should travel light in life's journey. Whatever slows our pace must be cast aside.

For me, at one point, being too quick to say yes to everything had become a heavy weight. This habit affected my personal life, my family life, even my church ministry. How about you? Your weights may be an excess of hobbies, television, internet information, poor time management, poor financial planning, or fear of rejection.

Take a look at the heroes of the faith in Hebrews chapter eleven. They are willing to throw off the weights that drag them down. They are our paradigms. Too much attachment to his home could have become a weight for Abraham. But love of his country did not stop him from seeking a better one with God's guidance. Nothing could hinder Enoch from walking with God. The writer of Hebrews describes Enoch as a man of faith who pleased God: "By faith Enoch … was commended as one who pleased God. And without faith it is impossible to please God, because anyone who comes to him must believe that he exists and that he rewards those who earnestly seek him" (Heb. 11:6).

The author talks about sin, which is the other type of weight: "If we deliberately keep on sinning after we have received the knowledge of the truth, no sacrifice for sins is left, but only a fearful expectation of judgment" (Heb. 10:26–27). Sin so easily entangles us, so easily captures us. We must watch for it carefully.

What about the sins that have already hindered us? What if we are unwilling to cast off our burdens? One of my burdens is complaining. I thought I was the best husband in the world. I made dinner and did housework. Did I really complain about my wife all the time? I didn't think so. I only thought of her as a woman who could be stronger in faith, especially when she questioned the visions and the dreams the Lord gave me. But my two boys told me I should speak to her more gently. That was when I remembered 1 Peter 3:7. "Husbands, in the same way be considerate as you live with your wives, and treat them with respect as the weaker partner and as heirs with you of the gracious gift of life, so that nothing will hinder your prayers."

The Israelites could not reach their promised land precisely because they were also complainers. They complained all the way through the wilderness. They clung to their misery, and that is why they perished in the desert. They never listened. And even when they listened, they did not believe.

There are other besetting sins which must be cast away: jealousy, greed, pride, lust of the flesh, and quickness to anger. The Lord commands us to remove all that hinders us. Matthew 5:29 says that "If your right eye causes you to sin, gouge it out and throw it away. It is better for you to lose one part of your body than for your whole body to be thrown into hell." What is Jesus trying to teach us here? It is that nothing should be so dear and precious to us that we must cling to it if it entangles us.

Are you willing to let go of the weights or sins that will prevent you from winning your life's race? If there is a price to pay, are you prepared? NFL Hall of Famer Ronnie Lott can tell you the sacrifice required of him to win just one game. He hurt his left pinky finger in 1985 when his team, the San Francisco 49ers, was playing the Dallas Cowboys. Nonetheless, he finished the rest of the game. After the season, he faced a challenging decision to either have an operation on the injured finger and miss the next season, or cut part of the finger off and continue playing. Ronnie Lott chose not to miss the next season, so he had part of his finger cut off. For most people, that would have been a tough decision. Yet even at the expense of losing some of his pinky finger, Lott decided that nothing would keep him from running the race marked out for him.[16] He said his father always told him to "exhaust life," and it's clear he followed his dad's advice.[17]

Fix Your Eyes on Jesus

The author of Hebrews gives us another principle for completing the race. He tells us to "fix our eyes on Jesus, the author and perfecter of our faith" (Heb. 12:2). In the third verse of Hebrews chapter twelve we are told to "consider him." How do we do that? We do that by thinking of the ways he conquered pain, endured the shame of the cross, and suffered persecution for sinful men and women. What great inner strength Jesus had! Think about how he faced Herod and Pilate before being crucified. Think about how he endured the mockery of people who said that if he were the Son of God he should be able to save himself. Jesus trusted God absolutely; only the Messiah is qualified to be the author and perfecter of his followers' faith. The same Holy Spirit who empowered Jesus will also invigorate Christians in the twenty-first century. In Christ, we all are winners of the races marked out for us.

In my years as a pastor, I have learned the secret of attaining joy. It is not a secret in the sense that it is hidden knowledge, but a secret in the sense that few have discovered it. It is simple: I maintain absolute obedience to God in every situation he places me in. To attain the joy awaiting him, Jesus endured all kinds of pain, both physical and spiritual. I should not do less. Once I woke up from a dream at midnight with tears flowing down my face. In the dream, someone kept falsely accusing me. I tried to defend myself, but the Lord did not allow me to do so. In fact, the Lord Jesus asked me to keep silent. As I was about to cry out to the Lord for justice, I heard a small voice telling me, "As Shimei cursed King David, so do I allow this fellow to do it to you." All of a sudden, my heart calmed and I woke. I reached for my Bible, turned to 2 Samuel 16:5–12 and I meditated on the following story:

> As King David approached Bahurim, a man from the same clan as Saul's family came out from there. His name was Shimei son of Gera, and he cursed as he came out. He pelted David and all the king's officials with stones, though all the troops and the special guard were on David's right and left … Then Abishai son of Zeruiah said to the king, "Why should this dead dog curse my lord the king? Let me go over and cut off his head." But the king said, "What do you and I have in common, you sons of Zeruiah? If he is cursing because the LORD said to him, 'Curse David,' who can ask, 'Why do you do this?'" David then said to Abishai and all his officials, "My son, who is of my own flesh, is trying to take my life. How much more, then, this Benjamite! Leave

him alone; let him curse, for the LORD has told him to. It may be that the LORD will see my distress and repay me with good for the cursing I am receiving today."

While meditating on the story, I cried out, "Lord, I am willing. Lord, I am willing to bear my own cross to follow you."

Exhaustion could have made me quit ministering to so many needy congregants. Each Monday I fought the desire to jump on a plane and escape to the beautiful beaches of Taiwan. I didn't, however, because I knew I had a higher calling. As I have stayed the course here in California, the Lord has strengthened me. And he will strengthen you. Run with perseverance the race God has put in front of you, and you will also be invited to become a hero of faith—to encourage others to trust in God's constancy. Together we run. Together we will all be in the Hall of Faith. Forever and ever. Amen.

And pray in the Spirit on all occasions with all kinds of prayers and requests. With this in mind, be alert and always keep on praying for all the saints.

—Ephesians 6:18

Chapter 7

TOGETHER WE PRAY IN THE SPIRIT

An elderly brother in Christ overheard his granddaughter repeating the alphabet with great sincerity. "What on earth are you up to?" he said. "I'm saying my prayers," she said. "But I can't think of exactly the right words tonight, so I'm just saying all the letters. God will put them together for me, because he knows what I'm thinking."[18] This girl didn't have the right words, but she had the right idea. She offered her letters, knowing the Spirit would make a prayer for her. There is no certain formula for praying in the Spirit. But if we too remind ourselves to submit to the Spirit, we can trust that the Lord is listening.

Praying in the Spirit

In Ephesians 6:18, Paul tells us to pray in the Spirit. "Pray in the Spirit on all occasions with all kinds of prayers and requests. With this in mind, be alert and always keep on praying for all the saints." Praying in the Spirit means we should not direct our appeal, but ask the Holy Spirit to do so on our behalf. Andrew Murray, a great prayer warrior, emphasized the need for utter dependency on the Holy Spirit when he wrote, "In every prayer the triune God takes a part—the Father who hears, the Son in whose name we pray, and the Holy Spirit who prays for us and in us."[19]

Andrew Murray has well stated that the Holy Spirit prays for us and in us. In Romans 8:26–27, Paul writes:

> In the same way, the Spirit helps us in our weakness. We do not know what we ought to pray for, but the Spirit himself intercedes for us with groans that words cannot express. And he who searches our hearts knows the mind of the Spirit, because the Spirit intercedes for the saints in accordance with God's will.

How encouraging! We are assured that the Holy Spirit is asking for what we do not even know we need.

A long time ago, my car broke down and I called AAA. Unfortunately, since I know very little about mechanics, I couldn't even describe the problem. When the technician dispatched by AAA arrived, he called his company and described the problem precisely. He used words I didn't even understand. Despite my ignorance, my needs were met, because someone communicated with the company on my behalf. This is what the Holy Spirit does for us. Even when we do not know what to say, the Holy Spirit does. He prays in a language that the Father understands perfectly.

The Holy Spirit is like a trustworthy lifeguard. Whenever we are in trouble he comes to help us, even when we do not know how to approach God. A man once asked a lifeguard, "How can you hear a person drowning when all these people are making noise on the beach with all the talking, yelling, whistling, and everything else?"

"I've been at this job for twenty years and I haven't let one person go on in distress," the lifeguard said. "My ears are tuned toward those in distress."[20] As a lifeguard is to those in distress, so the Holy Spirit is to those who are weak and helpless. We can trust in the Holy Spirit because he intercedes for Christians in accordance with God's will.

Jesus refers to the Holy Spirit as "Counselor" or "the Helper." As he tells, "I will ask the Father, and he will give you another Counselor to be with you forever—the Spirit of truth" (John 14:16–17). The actual Greek word he uses is *paraclete,* an ancient warrior's term. Greek soldiers went into battle in pairs so that when the enemy attacked they could draw together, back-to-back, covering each other's weak side.

One battle partner was the *paraclete* to the other. Our Lord does not send us to fight the good fight alone. The Holy Spirit is our battle partner who covers our blind side and fights for our well being. You are not alone. The Holy Spirit is taking an active role in helping you pray. Do you not feel like praying anymore? Do not hesitate or stop, but thank God instead, for this is the key moment. When you are tired of praying, that is the very moment that inclines you to humbly pray in the Spirit, since you are no longer depending on yourself!

Make Time

Faith requires action. Making time is as important as keeping in the Spirit. One of the main reasons we don't have significant prayer lives is not so much that we don't want them but that we don't plan them. If you don't plan a vacation, you will probably stay home and watch TV instead. Likewise, if you don't plan time to pray, you probably won't pray even once a day. An interviewer once asked people in a retirement home, "What do you find the most difficult thing to do here?"

He was surprised by what he heard. "To find time to read the Bible and pray."[21]

Schedule as many times as possible for prayer. Withdraw from the crowd. This is what Jesus did. I mentioned earlier that I find time in my daily schedule to meditate seven times. I consider meditation a form of prayer. The beauty of a schedule like this (which I have called the "four plus three" system) is that even when I'm not meditating, my mind is on my next appointment with God.

Someone is reported to have asked a concert violinist in New York's Carnegie Hall how she became so skilled. She said that it was by "planned neglect." What she meant was that she planned to neglect everything that was not related to her goal. Likewise, you have to neglect everything that isn't related to being close to the Lord.

What comes to mind when you hear the words "computer games"? If you have children, these two words are probably not your favorites. Games are all right so long as we don't abuse them. But often, people lose control and become addicted—and this is especially true of children. I've had to deal with this issue in my own household.

My two boys were not addicted to video games, but they did play more than I liked. The three of us agreed (at my insistence) that they needed to set some limits. I tried hard to convince them to explore other activities, but they wouldn't listen. So I prayed, day and night. I beseeched the Spirit with sighs and sometimes tears. Two years later, to my surprise, my older son had reduced the amount of time he spent on computer games so much that he even began playing the piano again. My younger son, a tenth grader at the time, suggested I set parental controls on his computer: no access after 10:00 P.M. except for homework. I thank God for the Holy Spirit's intercession and for answering my prayers.

Praying on All Occasions

The apostle Paul, who had much more devotion than anyone else, reminds us what we can do to practice continual prayer with "all kinds of prayers and requests." We must confess, thank, and meditate. I recommend a book by Dick Eastman entitled *The Hour That Changes the World*.[22] This is an excellent resource that contains a personal plan for practical prayer. Eastman suggests different kinds of prayer—from thanking God for his faithfulness to praising, waiting upon the Lord, confessing, using Scripture, and meditating. If we spend five minutes on each type of prayer, we can have an hour filled with a dynamic, creative prayer rather than one of rote recitation.

Before I came to the San Jose area to pioneer Fountain of Joy Prayer Church, the Lord showed me this book in a dream. I had no idea there was a book by this title. In the dream, I beheld a beautiful blue sky. Then the cover appeared, words gleaming. I am convinced that this is the foundation that God has anointed for teaching me, and perhaps you, how to pray. True, theoretically we do not need any book besides the Bible. Yet I also know that if God gives me a resource to use, I have no choice but to humbly accept it. I have found this conviction after seventeen painful years of not emphasizing prayer enough.

Praying for Others

When we pray in the Spirit, we have a heavenly imperative to intercede for others. The Bible tells us, "Pray for each other so that you may be healed" (James 5:16). Scripture also teaches us to "pray in the Spirit on all occasions with all kinds of prayers and requests. With this in mind, be alert and always keep on praying for all the saints" (Eph. 6:18). The saints represent a special category of believers who are chosen and set aside from the world. Thus, we should not forget to ask grace for all fellow believers. And although the Ephesians text does not include unbelievers, this does not mean we should neglect them.

How is it possible to pray for others, especially when we have so many needs ourselves? The answer lies in love. Through love we will pray for others, even people we consider beneath ourselves. One Roman officer begged Jesus to come heal his slave. Upon hearing of the officer's humility, Jesus said, "I haven't seen faith like this in all the land of Israel" (Luke 7:9). In his time, a slave could be traded as merchandise, yet the officer reached out to save him. This loving act pleased Jesus, who granted the request.

The Lord is looking for those among us with the same type of love as the Roman officer demonstrated. Motivated by love, we can offer mountain-moving prayers. Sooner or later, those for whom we are interceding will be blessed. Do you have someone in mind who needs salvation? Maybe your child, your parent, your neighbor, or someone who has been on your heart for a long time? Pray for him or her without ceasing.

Prayer in the Spirit, as Corrie ten Boom once put it, must be the steering wheel rather than the spare tire of our lives. By God's grace, I used the steering wheel for my two boys, and now my wife and I have seen their lives transformed. How about you? Be strong in the Lord and continue to pray in the Spirit.

The LORD is exalted over all the nations,
  his glory above the heavens.
Who is like the LORD our God,
  the One who sits enthroned on high,
who stoops down to look
  on the heavens and the earth?

He raises the poor from the dust
  and lifts the needy from the ash heap;
he seats them with princes,
  with the princes of his people.
He settles the childless woman in her home
  as a happy mother of children.

  Praise the LORD.

—Psalm 113:4–9

Chapter 8

TOGETHER WE ARE LIFTED

When Astronaut Edwin "Buzz" Aldrin, the second man to set foot on the moon, returned to earth, he quoted Psalm 8:3–4: "When I consider your heavens, the works of your fingers, the moon and stars, which you have ordained, what is man that you are mindful of him, the son of man that you care for him?" Seeing the universe with his own eyes and walking on the moon, Aldrin understood who controls the universe and what our place in that universe is. "O LORD, our Lord, how majestic is your name in all the earth! You have set your glory above the heavens" (Ps. 8:1).

Praise like this—enthusiastic and uncontrolled, instigated by wonder, admiration, and a sense of participation—is what our Lord wants from us. We praise the Lord not just because we are commanded to do so, however, but because he aids us here on earth.

From the Dust

In Psalm 113, we learn why the Lord is worthy to be praised. First, there is the majesty of the Lord, the sovereign God who is "exalted over all the nations, his glory above the heavens" (Ps. 113:4). And the psalmist gives another reason when he writes, "Who is like the LORD our God, the One who sits enthroned on high, who stoops down to look on the heavens and the earth?" (Ps. 113:4–5). In this psalm, we give praise to God because we learn that it is God who humbly bends to meet his creation with a tender heart. In every place, from the rising of the sun to its setting, from this time forth and forever, blessed be the name of the Lord. Hallelujah!

The psalmist then provides specific examples of how God stoops to care for us. In verses seven and eight he says, "He raises the poor from the dust and lifts the needy from the ash heap; he seats them with princes, with the princes of their people." Here we are shown how God takes care of the poor and the joyless. Neither can raise themselves out of the condition in which they are trapped. But God cares for them.

We have needs that we cannot meet by ourselves. There is only one thing God wants to do: raise us! And he always takes the initiative. Have you heard the story of David and Mephibosheth? In 2 Samuel chapter nine, David asked, "Is there anyone still left of the house of Saul to whom I can show kindness for Jonathan's sake?" Someone told him that Jonathan's son Mephibosheth was still alive, but crippled. There he was, a useless member of a despised family that had persecuted the reigning monarch. He had such low self-esteem that he even called himself a "dead dog" when he was brought before King David. He had no idea why the king was looking for him, but we can see that David was willing to help someone in need. Consequently, "Mephibosheth lived in Jerusalem, because he always ate at the king's table, and he was crippled in both feet" (2 Sam. 9:13). Likewise, God is willing to raise us. With God, we will be seated among the nobles.

When I was little, because my family was heavily in debt, I had to work outside the home and help my mother feed our pigs. Well, that was easy (it was fun to bathe them as well). The tough part was that I had to collect food for them. Back then, people left their dinner scraps in backyard buckets to be collected for the pigs. At one house after another, I collected them. The labor itself was nothing to me; I was used to working. It was the horrible smell that I couldn't accept. No matter how hard I tried to tighten the lid, my giant bucket still stank. The most painful part of this task, however, was that after I collected my scraps I carried them onto my father's company bus to go home. As soon as I got on, the other passengers covered their noses. Naturally, I felt bad for them, but the situation was also humiliating to me. Day after day, month after month, I developed low self-esteem and felt ashamed that people were sneering at me because of my background. To some degree I imagine I felt what Mephibosheth must have felt.

Such was my childhood, and many years passed before I became a Christian. That was when I learned the remarkable truth that God is willing to stoop to our level to save us. This wonderful grace of the Lord is something we do not deserve, yet the Lord lavishes it upon us all the same!

I heard a story when I became a Christian thirty-five years ago about a man from Europe who wanted to come to America. He used almost all his money to purchase a ship ticket, and since he had no money left to buy food on board, he filled his suitcase with cheese and crackers before boarding. On the ship, he saw all the other passengers eating in the large, ornate dining room. This poor fellow, however, isolated himself and ate his cheese and crackers. This went on every day of the voyage. The man could hear the other passengers enjoying the delicious food and joking about how they would need to go on diets. How he wished he could join them. Toward the end of the trip, someone approached him and said, "Sir, why don't you join us in the banquet hall and eat with us? You are always alone, eating cheese and crackers all the time."

"I only had enough money to buy my ticket; I had no money left for meals," he said.

"Sir, don't you know that meals are included in the price of the ticket?" the passenger asked. "Your meals have already been paid for!"

Can you imagine how the man felt after hearing this? He had suffered needlessly. Now, let me take you back to Mephibosheth. How many years did he waste in poverty, when all along he could have been receiving great blessings from King David instead? If only he had gone before David and claimed his rights under the covenant his father and King David jointly held, he would have received the king's favor much sooner.

Savor God's Grace

Do you know that God's grace is sufficient for you? The Lord told Paul "My grace is sufficient for you, for my power is made perfect in weakness. Therefore I will boast all the more gladly about my weaknesses, so that Christ's power may rest on me" (2 Cor. 12:9). In humility, Jesus descended to us from above.

Recently, I enjoyed reading *He Was Here,* a book that takes us back to the time when Jesus the Nazarene walked and worked on this very earth. From the Bethlehem innkeeper, to the prophetess Anna in the temple, to the man who was born without sight, thirty-three biblical characters appear in the book. What they have in common is that, despite their different backgrounds, they all encountered Jesus face to face.[23] Some decided to become his disciples, while others sought to harm him. While reading, I wondered whether I might have encountered Jesus myself and not even noticed. This book made me reflect on myself and how we all live. Since Jesus once stooped to serve, why do we still act as Thomas the doubter?

With this in mind, how often do you thank God for his grace? How often do you praise the Lord? Has the phrase "Praise the Lord" become your manner of life? If not, have you really tasted the grace of God in such a fashion that you feel compelled to praise him?

Psalm 113:9 says, "He settles the barren woman in her home as a happy mother of children. Praise the LORD." We see this in the Old Testament's account of Hannah and her encounter with the amazing grace of the Lord. Hannah took the initiative to come to Lord. Her husband loved her dearly and asked, "Why are you downhearted? Don't I mean more to you than ten sons?" (1 Sam. 1:8). Still, the barren Hannah was bitter in soul, and she wept much and prayed silently to the Lord. Her lips moved but her voice did not, so the high priest thought she was drunk. "Not so, my Lord," Hannah said, "I am a woman who is deeply troubled. I have not been drinking wine or beer; I was pouring out my soul to the LORD. Do not take your servant for a wicked woman; I have been praying here out of my great anguish and grief" (1 Sam. 1:15–16).

Many pilgrims had come and gone; some might have left a sacrifice but forgotten to offer a sincere prayer. But Hannah was different. She was a humble woman who wept before the Lord. Only in God can hopes be fulfilled! And Hannah's were.

God's grace likewise awaits us; we only need claim it. Why are you waiting? If you think there is nothing for which you can praise the Lord, try asking for something according to what he has promised in the Bible. We can praise God for miracles toward Hannah and the other heroes of the Bible, even though the miracles went to others rather than to us. God has certainly lifted me from the dust. Do you or someone you know need God's support? Remember you can find a reason to praise the Lord, since his grace is sufficient for all of us.

> Praise the Lord! Praise, O servants of the Lord. Praise the name of the Lord. Blessed be the name of the Lord from this time forth and forever. From the rising of the sun to its setting, the name of the Lord is to be praised.
>
> —Psalm 113:1–3

Praise the LORD.

Praise the LORD, my soul.

I will praise the LORD all my life;
  I will sing praise to my God as long as I live.
Do not put your trust in princes,
  in human beings, who cannot save.
When their spirit departs, they return to the ground;
  on that very day their plans come to nothing.
Blessed are those whose help is the God of Jacob,
  whose hope is in the LORD their God.

He is the Maker of heaven and earth,
  the sea, and everything in them—
  he remains faithful forever.

—Psalm 146:1–6

Chapter 9

TOGETHER WE SING PRAISES

I will never forget the last day of a biannual conference in Frankfurt, Germany, for Chinese Christian ministers from all over Europe. The only musical instrument we had for our worship was a guitar. To begin, the head pastor led us in singing the Chinese song "Jesus Loves You" with a gentle tempo. Naturally, I expected a faster song next. Ten minutes passed, but the pastor didn't change songs. He kept singing the same one to the melody of the guitar, slowing until it stopped completely. I thought this might be the best time for all of us to meditate on God's faithfulness and offer a prayer. Indeed, the pastor was leading the congregation in that very direction. Then, after a prayer, he raised his voice a little louder. He continued with the same song, still slow. Gradually, in tears, he led us into worship. I was still expecting him to change to another song. Then I stopped thinking about where I thought the worship should go, and tears burst from my eyes as I sang the simple, yet profound words from Colossians 1:13, "For he has rescued us from the dominion of darkness and brought us into the kingdom of the Son he loves." Jesus loves *me*. I knew we all meant what we sang. I believed we all sensed Jesus embracing us and touching our hearts. The pastor asked us to be seated. Another half an hour of worship passed. When I opened my eyes, everyone I saw was in tears.

Committing to Sing Praise

After the conference, I traveled toward Warsaw, where I was serving as a short-term missionary during a sabbatical from my ministry in San Jose. On the way back, I reflected on what I had experienced. Wasn't singing praises praying to God? I believe so. Doing so actually draws me closer to God because I am paying tribute to him. He is my only focus. Even in my weakness, I am devoting full attention to God's mighty character. Sometimes the beauty of piano, guitar, drum, and violin helps me dance through the trial, knowing the Lord is on the way, helping me.

"The LORD is my strength and my song; he has become my salvation. He is my God, and I will praise him" (Exod. 15:2). The Israelites sang these words with tambourines and dancing after the Red Sea divided, and thus, like them, we sing to glorify God. I resolved that, for all my life, I would sing exaltations to God in every situation.

The first two verses of Psalm 146 say "Praise the LORD. Praise the LORD, O my soul. I will praise the LORD all my life; I will sing praise to my God as long as I live." When we say "Praise the Lord! Hallelujah!" we should be aware that *hallel* means "praise," and it is in what we call the "imperative case." This simply means we are commanded to extol the Lord. The word "will" not only expresses future tense, it also shows determination. Here the psalmist invites us to share his strong conviction.

Not long after, my serious commitment to sing exaltations to God was put to the test. Heartbreaking news came from America. Living Hope, my church in San Jose, was falling apart. One after one, people left the church because they felt that as a shepherd I had abandoned them. Staying in Munich, I was so distressed when I heard this news that I found myself unable to pray or praise God. I was about to lose my congregation. How could I pray in such a situation? My "Living Hope" was dying. How could I sing? When I had been called to Poland, I was certain it was God's intention for me to leave my own church for a time, my own "flesh and blood," because I was fulfilling his call to help the Warsaw Christian Fellowship establish and build a church. Why, when I had come to help another church, had the Lord let mine crumble?

Throughout that night, I wrestled with God, asking why I had to suffer through this. My congregants had blessed my going to Europe in the name of Jesus. But if the Lord allowed them to leave, I must have done something wrong. Each face flew before my eyes, now gone, deserting me one by one. These thoughts spun in my head for hours.

At last, since I had committed to sing praises to God no matter what my situation, I picked up the songbook and tried. But I found I was too sad. Questions still raced through my head: Must I do something religious now? Can't I ring someone for a chat? Or maybe go watch a movie? Can't I take a night and just be a little human?

Finally, I surrendered. "Okay, Lord, I will do something devotional. I will at least try." After a moment of hesitation, flipping through the pages, I read a random song aloud to God. "As the deer panteth for the water, so my soul longeth after thee, You alone are my—" I had to stop there. "Indeed, you alone Lord. I am coming to you." Gradually, I could feel the love that flows from Calvary strengthening me. The light was shining upon my face. I knew something inside was transforming me.

Tears flowed down my cheeks. "Lord, I love you. Lord, I love you." I took a shaky breath. "You alone are my heart's desire." Then I found myself singing the last part: "And I long to worship thee." Then the chorus: "You alone are my strength, my shield ... And I long to worship thee."[24] Holding the songbook, still singing, I fell into a deep sleep.

Completely refreshed next morning, I truly understood the value of singing praises in any situation, for "He who sings prays twice!" Although I had almost been defeated, just by trying to recall all the faces of those who were leaving, I felt no more shame. The darkest night had been replaced with brightest morning through the renewal of God's faithfulness. I did not need to live under the shadow of the past. I was able to sing victorious songs to face tomorrow.

After returning to the United States, everything happened just the way I had anticipated. Living Hope Church, penniless, had been forced to close down. Congregants left. Only one family stood firm. I had no salary, and we had to rent a storeroom in order to restart the church. Yet here we are today; it is entirely the Lord's doing, and it is marvelous in our eyes. I therefore thank God and praise him. I know that our determination to sing praises was the key to building our church's faith.

Singing through Trials

That first Sunday in a tiny storeroom, people were nervous before the service. My father was there on his second visit, and since my wife Susan had a very bad cold, we had no pianist.

"No problem," I said to the congregation. "As long as we have the Lord to worship, nothing can stop us. Let's sing 'How Great Thy Art!' and 'Jesus is My Best Friend.'" We sang songs of worship, just as we will in heaven someday (though there, we won't need a piano!). Through our singing of praises, my father was brought to Christ at the most difficult time of my life, at a time when people thought me a failure. Indeed, he who sings prays twice. And he who sings praises will see his prayers answered.

In the twentieth chapter of Second Chronicles, the country of Judah faced attacks, and its people were dismayed. After consulting the people, King Jehoshaphat appointed men to walk out ahead of the army and sing praise to the Lord for the splendor of his holiness. "Give thanks to the LORD, for his love endures forever." What a brilliant military strategy, and in the end the Israelites won the battle. The Bible tells us, "As they began to sing and praise, the LORD set ambushes against the men of Ammon and Moab and Mount Seir who were invading Judah, and they were defeated" (2 Chron. 20:22). Later, the army assembled in a place they named the Valley of Beracah—The Valley of Praises. By singing praises, the soldiers were acknowledging that God was indeed their help and hope.

I know a beloved brother in Christ named David Kuo. David once lived in the United States but had to move back to Taipei to take care of his sick mother. Taking care of an ill family member is terribly painful. So how did he spend those difficult days? His sister told me that, for the entire last two years of his mother's life, David used to sing "Jehovah is my God" to her. The song quotes Psalm 3: "How many rise up against me! Many are saying of me, 'God will not deliver him.' But you are a shield around me, O LORD you bestow glory on me and lift up my head." Although he was singing to his mother, in reality, David was confirming the blessings God had given him all those years. Through this experience, his entire outlook brightened and he began reading the Bible at least an hour each day.

Do Not Trust Yourself, Trust God

"Blessed is he whose help is the God of Jacob, whose hope is in the LORD his God, the Maker of heaven and earth, the sea, and everything in them—the LORD, who remains faithful forever" (Ps. 146:5–6). Here in the psalm, we are reminded that our God is a powerful Creator and that he is always faithful. He is described as the God of Jacob, reminding us of his covenant. Throughout the Bible, we can see that through generation after generation, the God of Abraham, of Isaac, and of Jacob makes their descendents into a great nation. For this we proclaim his faithfulness with hundreds upon hundreds of gospel songs and hymns from "How Great Thou Art," and "Great Is Thy Faithfulness," to "As the Deer" and "You are my Hiding Place."

When you need help and look for hope, is the God of Jacob the One you are leaning on? Have you ever seen a technician climb an electrical pole? In the old days, technicians would insert two metal sticks in the holes of the pole to help them climb. The only thing that secured them was a safety belt attached to their waist, which they wrapped around the pole. Then they would alternate steps on the sticks and climb upward.[25] In life, can you trust God as the technician trusts his safety belt? Even as the psalmist praises God, he warns us to trust him above everyone on earth. When the psalmist warns us never to rely on any human being, what he is saying is that no human being has the power to do what God can do for us. We are weak, not Almighty, like God.

This past Monday evening, I knelt down in the kitchen before the Lord. I asked him to forgive me and asked him to help me stop being dependent on myself. Why was I so humble? At noon that day, I had had a car accident. I was too busy. I was swamped. I was rushing to do my errands, even though I had a strange feeling that something might go wrong. The Holy Spirit had warned me that I had no excuse for not taking the Sabbath seriously. But I didn't listen. I received an unexpected phone call and raced out the door. Driving too fast while answering my cell phone, I had a car accident. What happened? I was busy dialing. Then came the red light. Cars had already stopped there, but I thought I had enough distance between us. I was wrong and hit the car right in front of me. The accident could have been much more serious because the other car had a baby on board. Thanks to God's mercy, nothing bad happened. Can I be trusted? No! I am not capable of doing everything I know I should do.

Immediately after the accident, I did praise the Lord. When I passed the same spot the next day, I sang "Great is Thy Faithfulness" to him for punishing me and protecting me. I knew I needed to place my trust in God, not in myself. As the psalmist says, "Not to us, O LORD, not to us but to your name be the glory, because of your love and faithfulness" (Ps. 115:1). This, like all psalms, is meant to be sung. Singing helps us express our passion toward God. And as we offer our deepest selves up, we also offer our trust.

Today the Lord is calling us to trust him—to trust that he will give us blessings, abundant blessings. We sing praises not just because we have seen his mighty works, as Moses and the Israelites did in the parting of the Red Sea, but we also sing because, no matter what our circumstances, we put our simple faith in God.

Sing from the Heart

I wish I could just stop here and sing praises with you forever. I wish time could just stop, right here and now. How I wish for all of you to be blessed. "Blessed is he whose help is the God of Jacob, whose hope is in the LORD his God." In the Hebrew text, the "blessing" described in verse five of Psalm 146 is an "abundant blessing." The text is telling us that we will receive abundant blessings if we get help from God and put our hope in him.

In the New Testament, we read about Paul and Silas praying and singing hymns to God in prison at midnight, while other prisoners listened. Suddenly, there was a massive earthquake that shook the foundations of the prison. All the prison doors flew open, and every-one's chains came loose. Paul did not depend on any other human, but instead he trusted in God. His experience testifies to the power of singing praises. Sing along with the giants of faith. That is one of the best ways to help you focus only on God. Sing praises and expect abundant blessings in your life. This singing will certainly escort us to the throne of grace to receive all the blessings that have been reserved for us. Do you trust in Christ alone to bring you help and hope?

Vocal praise and songs of praises should be our daily dialogue with God. Orel Hershiser, a World Series MVP and Associated Press Professional Athlete of the Year, spoke of his triumphs: "I was singing hymns to myself to relax and keep my adrenalin down, because every time I thought about being ahead, I got too excited to pitch."[26]

The morning after winning the World Series, he was invited to be on *The Tonight Show*. Orel tried refusing to sing in public. Amidst audience cheering, Johnny Carson encouraged him. "This could be a first," he smirked.[27]

Orel began singing the hymn he had sung to himself between innings during the playoffs:

> Praise God from whom all blessings flow.
> Praise him all creatures here below.
> Praise him above ye heavenly hosts,
> Praise Father, Son, and Holy Ghost. Amen.[28]

On TV, Hershiser gave credit for his victories to God. Because he had offered his heart to God in the hymns he had sung, he knew God had answered his prayers. His mission now is to encourage us to sing along and enjoy the abundance of life in Christ. For him the baseball dugout became a field of praise, just as an ordinary valley became a valley of praise for King Jehoshaphat and his people. Where is your place of praise, the place from which the Lord's abundant blessings can flow upon you?

One day, a group of Christian teenagers gathered in a church to sing praises. The youth pastor came and told the group that he wanted to introduce a special friend of his named Charlie. Charlie had been born with a mental disability, but he loved Jesus and loved to sing to him. When the pastor called Charlie to the platform, some people squirmed uncomfortably. Charlie just didn't look "normal." But the pastor continued, telling the group that Charlie wanted to sing his favorite song, "Jesus Loves Me," for everyone there.

People watched as Charlie sang as if Jesus were in front of him. His singing was almost unbearable, and if they hadn't been told what he was going to sing, listeners wouldn't have been able to figure it out. But everyone knew that Charlie believed in every word he was singing. As the relater of this tale asks, "When God hears our praises, does he hear our voices or does he hear our hearts?" One thing everyone there knew for certain was that God loves it when Charlie sings.[29] Thank God we don't need to be great singers to please him. Thank God that as long as we are as innocent as children, we are in his presence. For, as Jesus teaches us, "Blessed are the pure in heart, for they will see God" (Matt. 5:8). God bless you all, and may you enjoy singing praises as much as Charlie does.

Now on his way to Jerusalem, Jesus traveled along the border between Samaria and Galilee. As he was going into a village, ten men who had leprosy met him. They stood at a distance and called out in a loud voice, "Jesus, Master, have pity on us!" When he saw them, he said, "Go, show yourselves to the priests." And as they went, they were cleansed. One of them, when he saw he was healed, came back, praising God in a loud voice. He threw himself at Jesus' feet and thanked him—and he was a Samaritan. Jesus asked, "Were not all ten cleansed? Where are the other nine? Was no one found to return and give praise to God except this foreigner?" Then he said to him, "Rise and go; your faith has made you well."

—Luke 17:11–19

Chapter 10

TOGETHER WE THINK
AND THANK

I was exhausted, but I dragged myself to my friend's special luncheon anyway. To my surprise it was a startup company presentation. Just as I was standing to slip out to my car, someone started to give a speech. I sighed and sat back down. Imagine my feelings when I discovered the speech was on cosmetics. "Do I really need to sit through a speech meant for ladies?" I thought. "They don't actually expect me to be here, do they?" I tried to find a decent excuse to leave, but as I listened to the speech, I found the words inspiring.

"The first step, the most important step, is to not put anything bad on your face," the speaker said. "Remove anything that will hurt your skin." Her words sounded like a sermon. The speaker, a cosmetician and CEO, was applying a great principle of her profession: To care for your skin, you must first stop using anything that might hurt it. Then you can add things that help to make you beautiful.

Remove an Ungrateful Heart

To have a beautiful life, remove the components that are harming you. Do you know what will harm your spiritual well-being? An ungrateful heart. This is what Jesus protested when he asked, "Was no one found to return and give praise to God except this foreigner?" (Luke 17:18). After Jesus cured ten men of leprosy, nine of them did not bother to return and thank God. Do we belong to this group? The entire Bible warns us of the serious consequences of forgetting the grace that God has shown us. If we focus on God, he will provide; if we focus on ourselves, we will be held accountable.

Consider the Old Testament figure of Saul, for instance. It's hard to read about the tragedy of his life. It's hard to see him die on the battlefield with his son Jonathan—one of the most admirable young men in the Bible. Wasn't Saul chosen by God? Yes! Wasn't he anointed king? Yes! Did God fail to keep him, to watch over him? No! But later the Lord could not be Saul's God anymore. Why? Because Saul forgot his humble origins once he prospered as a king. Samuel rebuked him, saying: "Although you were once small in your own eyes, did you not become the head of the tribes of Israel? The Lord anointed you king over Israel … To obey is better than to sacrifice" (1 Sam. 15:17, 22). How humble Saul was when he was first anointed king! At first, people could not even find him because he had hidden himself away among the baggage. But in his ungrateful heart, he allowed jealousy and insecurity to take root, which caused him to try to kill David and even his own son Jonathan. The God who had raised him was no longer his focus.

With his ungrateful heart, Saul chose to focus on himself, and so he was held accountable. Saul should have remembered the words of Moses:

> Be careful that you do not forget the LORD your God, failing to observe his commands, his laws and his decrees that I am giving you this day. Otherwise, when you eat and are satisfied, when you build fine houses and settle down, and when your herds and flocks grow large and your silver and gold increase and all you have is multiplied, then your heart will become proud and you will forget the LORD your God … You may say to yourself, My power and the strength of my hands have produced this wealth for me. But remember the LORD your God, for it is he who gives you the ability to produce wealth, and so confirms his covenant, which he swore to your forefathers, as it is today.
> —Deuteronomy 8:11–14, 17–18

Moses promises punishment for those who forget that God was the true provider of these blessings. As he warned the people of Israel, "Like the nations the LORD destroyed before you, so you will be destroyed for not obeying the LORD your God" (Deut. 8:20).

Blessings for a Grateful Heart

What happened to the one leper out of ten who returned to give thanks to Jesus Christ? Jesus told him, "Rise and go; your faith has made you well." Not only was he healed, he was made "well"—rescued from his leprosy and delivered from his sin. Only one leper out of ten received additional blessings from Jesus, not only temporary physical wholeness but also eternal blessings. The lesson is that whoever comes back to Jesus will always enjoy the spiritual blessings that no one can take away. The entire Bible tells us that in Christ we will have peace, joy, wisdom, grace, and power. Even faced with tragedy, we can endure it by remembering that the Lord will provide.

The poet Fanny Crosby reportedly wrote more than eight-thousand hymns. She became blind in infancy due to improper treatment of an eye inflammation caused by a common cold. When she heard that the man who had treated her was overcome with guilt, she said she would like to tell him, "Thank you, thank you for making me blind." She believed that, although the man might have made a mistake, God could not have. She believed that she had become blind because God wanted her to concentrate on praising him.

One day, she was visiting her dear friend Phoebe Knapp. Phoebe, after playing a tune for her, asked, "What does this tune say?"

"Why, that says, 'Blessed assurance, Jesus is mine.'"[30]

This hymn is still played today in thousands of churches. "Blessed assurance, Jesus is mine! O what a foretaste of glory divine … This is my story, this is my song, praising my Savior all the day long. This is my story, this is my song, praising my Savior all the day long."[31] How beautiful Fanny's life was. It is one of the most powerful testimonies to the beauty of life in Christ. Always come to Jesus Christ, and you too will see your life blossoming into one that is beautiful and powerful, a kind of life that you will never have if you remain ungrateful. When you are grateful, you remember that God can do what he has promised. A grateful heart enables you to focus on God alone—and not on anyone or anything else. As a reward, blessings will flow into your life.

Try Thanksgiving!

Maybe you agree with all of this in principle, but you just aren't sure how to show gratitude. Begin by talking about God whenever you see a new baby, a blue sky, or even a lightning storm. Thank him throughout the day. Surround yourself with items that help you focus on God. I brought back a drawing of the Wailing Wall from my first visit to Jerusalem. Now it hangs close to my garage door, reminding me of how when I first came to America, I didn't even own any personal items. And in eternity, whatever I have always belongs to God. I am only a steward in the kingdom.

What can you do to become grateful? Think and thank. In the Anglo-Saxon culture, to be "thankful" meant to be "thinkful." The phrase "Think and Thank" is inscribed in many English churches. Thinking of our blessings should stir us to gratitude.

Once, a missionary in China was living a seemingly hopeless life. For him everything was touched with melancholy. He tried hard. He prayed for a breakthrough. Yet he didn't improve. He finally left his work for a retreat where he could pray and overcome his pit of spiritual despair. When he reached his new station, he saw a motto on a fellow missionary's wall: "Try thanksgiving!" These two words caught his full attention and he thought, "Have I been praying all this time, but not praising?" He began thanksgiving, and his heart was lifted right away.[32]

Do you feel defeated? Think about something you can give thanks for. If you give thanks, do it publicly—that's what the grateful leper did when he threw himself at the feet of Jesus in thanksgiving. Leave yourself no room for being ungrateful.

We can learn a similar lesson from the Masai tribe in West Africa. When the Masai express thanks, they bow, put their foreheads on the ground, and say, "My head is in the dirt." And in another African tribe, members who want to express gratitude sit for a long time in front of the hut of a person who has done them a favor and say, "I sit on the ground before you."[33] How humble! How sincere! How pure in heart! If they are willing to offer such a public display of thanks to fellow humans, how much more eagerly should we publicly thank God for all he has given us? And if Jesus died for us publicly, surely we can thank him publicly. Doing so will strengthen our faith.

Before my mother passed away from stomach cancer, I asked God to heal her. I begged God, saying I was willing to do anything for him if only he would heal my mother. Later, after she passed away, I got a cassette from Taiwan. Recorded on it was my illiterate mother's will. It said: "My son, do not force God! He has a will that we can't understand. Two things you should remember. First, don't owe people money. If you do, pay it back as soon as you can. The other is always be kind to everyone! Always! And remember, Jesus loves us." Her words were filled with love and thanksgiving. All her married life, she had worked hard to pay off the debts my father owed. Yet she did not complain. She stayed close to God and she thanked him continually.

If you believe you can feel grateful, even at times when it does not seem possible, then you will always have an antidote for discouragement or frustration. A tale tells of a man who happened upon a barn where Satan hoarded his seeds. Among many kinds, the seeds of discouragement were the most numerous. Why? This type of seed can grow almost everywhere. Satan, however, was forced to reveal that there was one place seeds of discouragement could never thrive.

"And where is that?" the man said.

"In the heart of a grateful man," Satan said sadly.[34]

The Lord knows there are seeds of discouragement that bring us down, so he has prepared an antidote. May gratitude become your attitude toward life.

Count Your Blessings

While Pastor Jack Hinton was on a short-term missionary trip, he led worship at a leper colony on the island of Tobago. There was a woman who had been facing away from the pulpit, but when she turned around, he saw, as he said, "the most hideous face I had ever seen." Her nose and ears were entirely gone. She lifted a fingerless hand in the air and asked Pastor Hinton if they could sing "Count Your Blessings." After singing the song, Pastor Hinton remained overcome with emotion as he led the service. Then a team member said, "I guess you'll never be able to sing that song again."

"Yes, I will," Pastor Hinton said. "But I'll never sing it the same way."[35]

Since the first time I heard this story, I have been determined to sing the song differently. I will humbly, sincerely count each and every single blessing I receive from the Lord. Whenever I can, I will give thanks to God in public. Let us all sing this song "differently" from before:

> When upon life's billows you are tempest tossed,
> When you are discouraged, thinking all is lost,
> Count your many blessings. Name them one by one.
> And it will surprise you what the Lord hath done.
> Count your blessings. Name them one by one.
> Count your blessings. See what God hath done!
> Count your blessings. Name them one by one.
> And it will surprise you what the Lord hath done.[36]

When it was almost time for the Jewish Passover, Jesus went up to Jerusalem. In the temple courts he found men selling cattle, sheep and doves, and others sitting at tables exchanging money. So he made a whip out of cords, and drove all from the temple area, both sheep and cattle; he scattered the coins of the money changers and overturned their tables. To those who sold doves he said, "Get these out of here! How dare you turn my Father's house into a market!" His disciples remembered that it is written: "Zeal for your house will consume me."

—John 2:13–17

Chapter 11

TOGETHER WE REBUILD THE PRAYER CHURCH

The "cleansing of the temple" is attested in every gospel account. But when did it happen? In Matthew, Mark, and Luke, the cleansing happens on Palm Sunday, immediately after Jesus' entry into Jerusalem. In the gospel of John, however, this event is so important and symbolic that it is described as one of the first things Jesus did in his ministry. So when did it happen? Was it in the beginning or at the end of Jesus' ministry? Or did this event happen more than once? No one knows. While opinions differ among the critics, I personally favor John Warwick Montgomery's view. He explained that, considering the condition of the temple in the first century, he would be surprised if Jesus didn't cleanse it every Saturday night.

How was it possible that Jesus, a supposedly mild-mannered, caring person, would act in such a violent way? Why was he so concerned about cleansing the temple? Some Christians still wonder. But the disciples of Jesus give us the answer. After Jesus cleansed the temple, they remembered what was written in Psalm 69:9: "Zeal for your house will consume me" (John 2:17). What kind of zeal was this? It was zeal for a temple where priests functioned properly to intercede for God's people. It was zeal for a temple where people could worship God freely. It was zeal for a temple where people of all nations could pray. Yet sadly, in Jesus' time, people could no longer experience God in the temple without being interrupted, since our Father's house had been turned into a chaotic market (John 2:16). Mark 11:17 tells us that, after the cleansing, Jesus said: "Is it not written: 'My house will be called a house of prayer for all nations?' But you have made it 'a den of robbers.'"

Restoring the Temple

Turned into a market, degraded into a den of robbers, the temple had lost its true function. Imagine you are a pilgrim who has longed to visit Jerusalem, maybe just once a year. Traveling day and night, perhaps singing some psalms—Psalm 120, Psalm 121, or Psalm 122—climbing over hills, you finally arrive in Jerusalem. How anxious you must be to restore your relationship with God. Consumed by joy and excitement, you rush into the temple. But what do you see there? A bazaar!

You are utterly discouraged and don't feel you are in a sanctuary of God. You can't focus and offer a sincere prayer at all, because people are yelling, "Get out of my way, you're taking my space." Goats and sheep are bleating. Doves are cooing. Oxen are lowing. And coins are rattling. Animal hair floats in dusty clumps. The smell of dung hangs heavily in the air. After working hard to save money for your pilgrimage, you find yourself unable to enjoy God's presence in the temple. How you would long for the restoration of the temple to its pure purpose so you could come to God there. How you would wish you could offer sincere prayers in the temple, uninterrupted!

Suddenly you hear someone say, "My house will be called a house of prayer for all nations." You may be surprised, but you are not shocked. At last, someone is protesting on your behalf. If even an ordinary pilgrim like you wished to see the temple restored, how much more would Jesus? This was his Father's house! He knew clearly that the temple service was no longer what his Father wanted it to be.

The moneychangers changed pilgrims' money from Roman coins into temple tokens that could be used to make purchases and pay for goods in the temple, and moneychangers and priests took a portion of the profits. In Mark 12:40, Jesus accused the teachers of the law of "devouring the widows' houses" through these practices.

Perhaps not all those who served in the temple meant to do evil. Maybe the moneychangers and the merchants who sold sacrificial animals simply intended to offer a convenience to pilgrims who couldn't take cattle or sheep with them while traveling. But whatever their intentions, they distracted people. This is what concerned Jesus the most. He wanted to destroy all the barriers that separated the pilgrims from God. No wonder John did not portray Jesus as a gentle teacher with a tender heart in this story. On the contrary, John showed him as a fiery Old Testament prophet who had come to turn the whole world upside down.

The Fountain of Joy

R. A. Torrey was one of the great American Bible teachers from the middle of the nineteenth century to the first part of the twentieth. He and his wife Clara went through a time of great pain and sadness when their twelve-year-old daughter died. The funeral was held on a gloomy, rainy day. They stood around the grave and watched as the coffin of their little girl was lowered.

"I'm so glad that Elisabeth is with the Lord, and not in that box," Mrs. Torrey said as they turned away.

But even knowing this to be true, their hearts were broken. Dr. Torrey said that the next day, as he was walking down the street, the magnitude of the experience broke upon him anew—the loneliness of the years ahead without the daughter's presence, the heartbreaking feeling of being in an empty house, and all the other implications of the daughter's death. He was so burdened by this that he looked to the Lord for help. He described what happened next:

> And just then, this fountain, the Holy Spirit that I had in my heart, broke forth with power such as I had never experienced before. It was the most joyful moment I had ever known in my life! Oh, how wonderful is the joy of the Holy Ghost! It is an unspeakably glorious thing to have your joy not in things about you, not even in your most dearly loved friends, but to have within you a fountain ever springing up, springing up, springing up, and springing up every single day of your life, year after year, springing up under all circumstances unto everlasting life![37]

A fountain of joy ever springing up, every day, to everlasting life! The entire gospel of John is inviting us to enjoy a life that will spring up in joy. Can you taste the joyful life now? Or are you still so distracted by everyday noise that you can't come to God with a pure heart? Are you ready for Jesus to come into your life with a whip? It seems to me that we need Jesus to be No More Mr. Nice Guy. By cleansing the temple, the Lord was waking everyone, including you and me, to the truth that the first thing we need to do in our lives is restore our relationship with God so we can taste joy in a world full of sorrow and pain.

Rebuilding the Church

I believe the Holy Spirit is calling us to rebuild the church as a prayer church, like Jesus was trying to rebuild the temple. Jesus' shout brings us back to God's desire as expressed in Isaiah 56:7: "These I will bring to my holy mountain, and give them joy in my house of prayer ... for my house will be called a house of prayer for all nations." Yes, as long as we are willing to cleanse ourselves, refocus on God, and restore our relationship with him, we will taste joy, no matter our circumstances.

After returning from my ministry trip to Poland, I was confronted with the most devastating situation a pastor can face—due to declining membership, my church, Living Hope, would have to close. Nevertheless, I told my wife Susan that we should stay, because even though Living Hope Church was gone, the Lord had promised me he would raise it from the dead. Then I told her the church's new name, which the Lord had shown me in prayer: Fountain of Joy Prayer Church. She looked at me as if I were a lunatic. How could I be the pastor of Fountain of Joy Prayer Church? *There was no church.* The congregation had left. Anyone would think I would feel despondent in a situation like this. But I told Susan that it was the Lord who had shown me the name of the church and that she needed to have faith that the church would be resurrected. Devastated, she burst into tears. She pleaded with me to go back to Europe, and since she was so hopeless, I almost agreed.

But instead I told her that I wanted to go back there someday, but not in a situation like this: "What am I going to tell the people in Europe? That I have come to help them because my church in the U.S. is gone?"

Although I tried to act strong and determined before my wife, I also needed to be alone to cry. I knew my life needed to rebuilt, and who could really rebuild it? It was Jesus, my precious Lord, who called me and offered to help me. And in turn, I had to be willing to be cleansed.

When I went downstairs to pray in solitude, to cry out for the Lord's divine guidance, something incredible occurred. A surge like electricity suddenly flowed through my body from head to toe. I had never felt such a sensation before. Miraculous power filled my body. I jumped so high that I almost hit my head against the kitchen ceiling.

"Hallelujah!" I shouted over and over. Susan thought that I had really gone crazy. We were so poor that we didn't even have the money to buy milk for our two boys. How could I be so joyous? But before long, Susan realized that the sensation I had experienced must have been real. Seeing the confirmation God had shown me, she agreed to help me restart the Fountain of Joy Prayer Church.

Remove Obstacles

What does all this have to do with us? Perhaps you think there is no corruption within you or that your church is functioning properly. Still, there is much to learn from the temple cleansing. When there is anything that can distract you from seeking God, you must dispose of it the way Jesus disposed of the moneychangers with his whip! Ask the Lord Jesus to strengthen you and remove all obstacles. The temple economy was a barrier to those who wished to enter the temple to pray. Likewise, some of the things in your life have blocked you from getting close to God. What old systems do you need to remove? Is there anything you can think of that would hinder you or the church from building the right relationship with God? What old systems do we as a church need to remove so that people can come to God with a pure heart? Some of these things may be good, or even very good in themselves. It's just that they are not supposed to be in our lives at the present. They have become obstacles without our being aware of it.

Recently I made the decision to remove the basketball hoops in the prayer garden at Prayer Church. We want people to come to our prayer garden to pray, not to play. It was a very painful decision for me, one that I avoided making for two years. Through my office window, I could see people having a great time playing basketball. But in order for more people to have access to the prayer rooms on Sunday, the hoops had to be removed. We thought more about playing ball in the garden than praying in it. They had become an obstacle.

Renew Your Life

When remodeling a business, the owner puts up a sign: "Closed for renovation." In like manner, are you ready to set yourself aside for renovation? Can you reorganize your private life now? Why not start with time spent on TV? Or online chats. Or text messages. Or phone calls. Remove anything that hinders you from strengthening your relationship with God. Ask God to point out your obstacles and then remove them one by one.

On the garbage can at a local Burger King™, I read a sign: "Toss it in. Drop it in. Slide it in off the tray. Just get your trash in here someway." Likewise, God has provided a place for you to toss, drop, or slide all the items that should be put away. Please do not misunderstand. I don't intend to say that what you treasure is trash. I am trying my best to convince you to put these cattle and sheep out of your life in the same way you toss, or drop, all trash.

You cleanse a temple so it functions properly, so worshippers can rejoice there. But you must do more than enter the temple to experience joy. First, you must pray.

I know it's easy to become distracted, but make prayer your priority. You can answer e-mails later. Take a break instead. Take a walk around the room or step outside for some fresh air. If possible, meditate on God's Word or think about his love. Schedule some "Jesus and you time." Go into your calendar and block off a period of time for uninterrupted daily devotion.

The other day I was giving my son a ride and listening to the classical FM music radio station. The announcer was interviewing a gifted ten-year-old violinist.

"Do you feel lost when you see others watching TV?" the announcer said.

"Well, I can't compare myself with others because I have never watched TV," the boy said. "Never have, never will. I don't know how to compare. However, I do enjoy some classic movies on video at home. You name it, I know it; I know them all."

The point is not that watching TV is bad. Indeed, some TV programs are good and you do not want to miss them. The point is that, in order to succeed in whatever you are entrusted, you have to free yourself from interruptions. Just as that young violinist could not both watch TV and at the same time practice the violin, so you cannot pray and be interrupted at the same time.

Devote Time to Real Prayer

A long time ago I discovered that when I am insufficiently focused, I enjoy the melody or words of a song so much that I no longer fully devote myself to prayer. Have you ever heard the "The Prayer" by Australian idol Anthony Callea? "I pray you'll be our eyes, and watch us where we go ... guide us with your grace to a place where we'll be safe. La luce che tu hai ... nel cuore restera ..."[38] It's seductively easy to love the melody and ignore the message. A song should lead us to God, not to distraction—this is what I keep on saying to myself. We must make sure there is no idol anywhere, whether a person or a great song. That way, we can really be free to worship and pray to God.

"A world where pain and sorrow will be ended. And every heart that's broken will be mended."[39] "The Prayer" speaks beautifully about ending sorrow and pain, and those words are God's promise, not to those who are merely caught up in the beauty of the song, but to those who really pray. Can you imagine how sad the Lord is when you are distracted by all the beautiful music he has given you, and cannot offer a true prayer? Do *not* allow anything, even something wonderful, to hinder your approaching God. Allow Jesus to cleanse you, whatever it costs.

Thank God, as long as we pray sincerely, in faith, our prayer will be answered. And he promises that, if we come and pray, he will make us rejoice. Let's claim the joy the Lord has promised us.

And here is my advice about what is best for you in this matter: Last year you were the first not only to give but also to have the desire to do so. Now finish the work, so that your eager willingness to do it may be matched by your completion of it, according to your means. For if the willingness is there, the gift is acceptable according to what one has, not according to what he does not have.

—2 Corinthians 8:10–12

Chapter 12

TOGETHER WE CAN DO IT NOW

When I graduated from the seminary in Tulsa twenty years ago, I was at a loss regarding how to move on with my life. I knew in spirit that God wanted me to come to the Bay Area. Still, I could not make the decision right away. Graduating seminary had meant studying from seven in the morning to eleven at night, while working part-time as a janitor. By the time I got my degree, I was so frail from liver disease that I could not even drive for more than half an hour. I had been bedridden for almost six months. With all this weighing me down, my doctor warned me against moving and pioneering a church. One Chinese pastor warned me that I had every reason to fail. Besides my poor health, I was not well-known, and I lacked ministry experience. In addition, since Chinese culture reveres the elderly, I was considered too young to be respected. Nonetheless, I knew God wanted me in the Bay Area. What should I do?

A Message from the Lord

After agonizing for several months, I still had no answer. One evening, I was wandering around the living room in our modest, one-bedroom apartment, seeking God's response to my question. Suddenly,

I recalled a note I had received from one of my acquaintances at church. During a meeting exploring the feasibility of building a new church in Los Angeles or the Bay Area, an elderly man had scribbled something on a piece of paper and slipped it into my church bulletin. Since he handed me the bulletin during prayer, I didn't open it on the spot, thinking that I would read it later. But when I got home, I had completely forgotten about it.

Now I was getting an urgent sense that, somehow, it contained a message to me from the Lord. But I could not remember where I'd left it. I offered my prayers to him, saying: "Forgive me for storing things improperly. Please show me where the bulletin is, if you truly have a message for me." Right after I prayed, I saw the bulletin stuck between my bed and the end table. It was hardly visible. Anxiously, I unfolded it and saw that the man had written, "May the Lord be with you," and then he referenced 2 Corinthians 8:10–12.

> And here is my advice about what is best for you in this matter: Last year you were the first not only to give but also to have the desire to do so. Now finish the work, so that your eager willingness to do it may be matched by your completion of it, according to your means. For if the willingness is there, the gift is acceptable according to what one has, not according to what he does not have.

Suddenly, I understood what that elderly gentleman had been trying to tell me through these verses. Tears stung my eyes. At that critical moment, the peace of Christ filled my heart. I had no doubt that the Lord wanted me to come to the Bay Area, no matter what others might say or think, no matter how young or frail I was.

Curious, I called the man to find out why he had left these verses for me. He told me that, while Pastor Budd and the others were praying for me that day, the Holy Spirit had urged him to bless me with those words. Having handed me the note, he completed his mission, and afterwards he had no recollection of the incident. I knew I had to faithfully accomplish my mission.

A year later, in obedience to God's will, I moved to the Bay Area with my family. Our older son, Suming, was two years old, and my wife was expecting our second son, Sukai. And of course, there was Jesus Christ. Since he was leading the way, I considered him part of our family, too. Praise the Lord, twenty years later, here and now, I can testify to the truth that the Lord showed me through those verses in Corinthians. God directs and guides through his Word. No matter how life's circumstances may change, no matter what may happen, God's message will never alter.

Unite and Give

I'm sure you all remember the terrible 2008 earthquake in Sichuan, China. The earthquake rescue missions brought many touching stories to the world's attention. In one story in particular, a three-month-old baby had slept through the earthquake peacefully, as if she were still sleeping in her mother's arms, even though her mother was killed. Realizing that the building she and her baby were in could collapse at any moment, she had stretched out her own body as fully as possible to cover her baby. Can you believe it? The mother's body was stronger than the collapsing building's cement pillars. What is more, in her dying moment, she left a text message on her cell phone: "Dear Baby, if you survive, please remember I will always love you."[40] When doctors and rescuers saw the message, they were so touched they froze in place. This brave mother had saved her baby from the collapsing building by sacrificing her own life!

People from all over the world united to help the earthquake rescue mission. Jackie Chan donated ten million RMB.* President-Elect Ma of Taiwan hosted a TV show to collect donations, even though it was a day before his inauguration. We may not have as much money to give as Jackie Chan, and we may not be as influential as President Ma, but as long as we give willingly, according to our individual situation, our gift is acceptable.

In the midst of this tragedy, during one of the biggest natural disasters in history, *Time* magazine's cover was captioned "China Stands

---

*Renminbi, the official currency of the People's Republic of China.

Up!" Before the earthquake, the world had watched China as she dealt with the tensions surrounding the Olympic Games and the issue of Tibet. But after the big earthquake, the world was amazed by how the Chinese worked hand in hand to rescue their people.

This is exactly what Paul tries to explain to the wealthy church in Corinth, when he urges them to accomplish what they have pledged—to help the needy in Jerusalem. Paul asks the Corinthians to open their hearts, since the Lord has laid this burden on them already. How can we do anything less regarding the people the Lord has laid on our hearts? This is exactly what the Bible wants to tell us today: "Christians stand up! Christians stand up!" How I wish this could be the headline on all the newspapers in the world.

Offer What You Have

Recall the story of Jesus and the five loaves and two fishes (Matt. 14:13–21, Mark 6:31–44, Luke 9:10–17, John 6:5–15). Night came, and there were thousands of hungry people to feed. The only food on hand, however, was five loaves of bread and two fishes, which belonged to a young boy who willingly offered them to the crowd. But how could five loaves and two fishes possibly feed thousands? Jesus, upon hearing what the boy had done, came and blessed his gift. Then, miraculously, there was enough food to feed everyone. The story of the loaves and fishes is the only miracle story told in its fullness in all four Gospels.

Over and over, we hear touching stories of how people bring only what they have, and then Jesus blesses them and multiplies their gifts. At the entrance to the garden in our own Fountain of Joy Prayer Church, stones on the ground depict five loaves and two fishes. The stones are leftovers from the paving work we did in the garden, laid out to remind us of what Lord Jesus can do if we offer what we have, even if we cannot offer much. When the Lord inspired us to pave the ground to make a prayer garden, we had less than a hundred dollars to spend, and we needed one hundred thousand. Little by little, after the first small donation, more and more donations came in. Eventually, God provided all that we needed to build our beautiful garden. God's hands were truly upon us.

Paul reminded the Corinthian church that everything flows from God's grace when he said, "I am not commanding you, but I want to test the sincerity of your love by comparing it with the earnestness of others. For you know the grace of our Lord Jesus Christ, that though he was rich, yet for your sakes he became poor, so that you through his poverty might become rich" (2 Cor. 8:8–9). As the song of worship puts it, "What can we give that you have not given? And what do we have that is not already yours ... Lord, I offer my life to you."[41] Are you willing to offer whatever God puts in your heart? "Remembering the words the Lord Jesus himself said: 'It is more blessed to give than to receive'" (Acts 20:35).

Wanting to help others, a young boy wrote a letter to Mother Teresa, asking how. It took months for him to receive the reply from Calcutta, India. Anxiously, he opened it, to find only four words: "Find your own Calcutta."[42]

Because of her unconditional obedience to the Lord, Mother Teresa rescued orphans and inspired millions on behalf of Christ. She had faith that God would show her the path she needed to follow. We can access that same faith. Where is your Calcutta?

My mother's Calcutta was her own humble family. Holding three jobs a day for thirty years and paying most of the gambling debts my father had accumulated, she raised three children with strong characters. Though we had to work all day, my mother always gave to a beggar, even if it was just a few pennies. Even after four of her seven children died in accidents, she finished the task with which God had entrusted her. With her unconditional obedience, she has become my role model as I complete my daily tasks given by God.

When I was in elementary school, I traveled to the local golf course at 4:30 A.M. each day in order to caddy. In junior high, I loaded trucks with watermelons and carried bags of cement that weighed fifty kilograms.

Before Susan and I were married, my brother jokingly asked if she was sure she wanted to marry me. Susan seemed a little surprised.

"Watch out!" my brother said. "My brother is the type of person who will invite people for dinner even when there is no rice at home."

Ah! It was true. But in all these years, Susan and I have always had what we needed. In Christ, there is always enough grace for us. More than enough. My mother taught me to do exactly what Lord Jesus did. And this is the advice I would like to pass on to you. Offer what you have. I want to encourage you to give, for being asked to give is the beginning of blessings. Since high school, I have always treasured the chance to give more than a tithe. Do I lack anything as a result? By God's grace, my family always has had more than we deserve. More than enough. God's grace is amazing. You can never surpass God in giving. You cannot outgive God.

Do It Now!

The apostle Paul encouraged Christ's followers in Corinth to be givers. Since they had been called to serve, they should have been willing to give cheerfully. Paul reminded them that even when experiencing severe trials, the Macedonian churches had donated even beyond their ability and pleaded to keep helping those in need. Paul is telling us here how the Lord seeks those with cheerful hearts.

Wei-Yi, one of my college classmates, was killed in a car accident. After his funeral, we went to his dormitory to pack his belongings and send them back to his family. To our surprise, we found out that he had been supporting three orphans. None of us knew. None of us knew our dear brother had begun the work Christ wants us to do, giving what he had to support others. While packing Wei-Yi's belongings, with tears rolling down our faces, we were convinced of the saying, "The things we'll do tomorrow are the things we would have done today if we had thought about them yesterday."

We are left with one final command. Paul tells us to "finish the work." He was anxious to see that the needs of the people in Jerusalem were met promptly. How could he watch some suffer while others intentionally delayed in answering God's call? He knew he had to remind—to urge—people to do good. Unless people are motivated, nothing can be accomplished.

We can learn much from the earthquake rescue missions in China. The Chinese government wanted everyone to have a shelter within one month. If you had watched the news, you would have seen the eyes of the workers who were making the tents. They did not want to procrastinate. They *wanted* to do what they were doing, with what they had, and with cheerful hearts.

To my own congregation, I am calling for us to participate more in our church. Are you willing to spend just one hour a week working for your church and spreading the Word? That is how churches grow. Start with someone you know. Go visit your friends and relatives and tell them about God's love. Invite someone for dinner. Let him know you care that he comes to church to enjoy the abundant life we can find in Christ.

At last, we are fulfilling our mission to plant new churches and help them grow. We have already received such enormous help building a brand-new church, this time in South San Jose. When we were searching for a location, God opened the door for us to ask another church about their building's availability. We are grateful that Pastor Dan and others there were so gracious to us. Cheerfully, kindly, they offered what they had, and they agreed that we could use their facility.

After we had been using it a few weeks, as I drove to the church from a different direction, I suddenly realized it was on exactly the same street as my first church, Living Hope—the one that had closed down. With tears, I said, "Jesus, I love you. I thank you for giving me a second chance to come back here, a place I otherwise would have wanted to avoid. Lord, thank you! You heard me cry ten years ago when I asked you to bring me back here to plant another church. Now I can testify to others who fail in their undertakings that our God is a God of second chances."

FINAL WORDS OF ENCOURAGEMENT

This collection of sermons was given at Fountain of Joy Prayer Church, once Living Hope Church, which was raised from the dead through the Lord's mercy and grace. The congregation there accepted me as an imperfect person and together we grew in faith. I believe what my small congregation has done for me, you can do with your church and your pastor. While you ask your pastor to shepherd you, your pastor needs your encouragement.

My heart's desire is to see my fellow Christians rooted in spirituality and branching out with ministries. From finding hope in Christ to growing in faith to bearing the torch of the gospel, you can experience the faithfulness of God, the power of the Good News. Together we can do it now. No matter where your church is, together we can advance the gospel. "He who began a good work in you will carry it on to completion until the day of Christ Jesus" (Phil. 1:6).

ENDNOTES

1. "The Sky Angel Cowboy," Online Movie (Nebraska: Christian Broadcasting Network, December 24, 2007) YouTube™, LLC, http://www.youtube.com/watch?v=C0r_FbARIn8.
2. Charles Colson, "It Really Didn't Matter," in *Stories for the Extreme Teen's Heart,* ed. Alice Grey (Sisters, Ore.: Multnomah, 2000), 63–64.
3. Sheri Rose Shepherd, *Life Is Not a Dress Rehearsal* (Sisters, Ore.: Multnomah, 2000), 173–175.
4. Rebecca Manley Pippert, "Ellie and Rolf," in *Stories for the Extreme Teen's Heart,* ed. Alice Grey (Sisters, Ore.: Multnomah, 2000), 101–102.
5. Author Unknown, "The Story of the Praying Hands," in *Stories for the Extreme Teen's Heart,* ed. Alice Grey (Sisters, Ore.: Multnomah, 2000), 168–169.
6. John F. Walvoord, *Philippians: Triumph in Christ, Everyman's Bible Commentary* (Chicago: Moody, 1971), 49–50.
7. Bob Brown, "Born without Limbs, Refusing Limitations: Using His Voice, Preacher Nick Vujicic Inspires People Around the World," *ABC News,* Health Section, March 27, 2008, http://abcnews.go.com/Health/story?id=4531209&page=1.

8. Julian Keith Getty and Stuart Richard Townend, "In Christ Alone," Gospel Hymn, 2002.

9. Richard Marosi and Tony Perry, "Man Mourns Family's Loss, Forgives Pilot in Jet Crash," *Los Angeles Times*, Local, December 10, 2008, http://articles.latimes.com/2008/dec/10/local/me-jetcrash10

10. Max Lucado, *The Applause of Heaven* (Nashville: Thomas Nelson, 1999), 6–7.

11. Michael P. Green, *Illustrations for Biblical Preaching* (Grand Rapids: Baker, 1991), 371.

12. Roy B. Zuck, *The Speaker's Quote Book* (Grand Rapids: Kregel, 1997), 376.

13. *Chariots of Fire*, DVD (1981; USA: Warner Home Video, 2007).

14. Roy B. Zuck, *The Speaker's Quote Book* (Grand Rapids: Kregel, 1997), 286.

15. Stephanie Chen, "Paralyzed Shooting Victim Competes in Marathons," *CNN*, Justice, April 16, 2010, http://articles.cnn.com/2010-04-16.

16. Ronnie Lott, *Total Impact* (New York: Doubleday, 1991), 110–123.

17. Ronnie Lott, Interview by Jerry Kavanagh, "The *Daily* Goes One-On-One With Pro Football HOFer Ronnie Lott," *Street & Smith's Sports Business Daily*, January 31, 2008, https://www.sportsbusinessdaily.com/article/118099

18. Roy B. Zuck, *The Speaker's Quote Book* (Grand Rapids: Kregel, 1997), 298.

19. Andrew Murray, "The Prayer Life 6: The Holy Spirit and Prayer," oChristian.com, accessed September 2, 2010, http://articles.ochristian.com/article1894.shtml

20. Roy B. Zuck, *The Speaker's Quote Book* (Grand Rapids: Kregel, 1997), 296.

21. Ibid., 300.

22. Dick Eastman, *The Hour that Changes the World* (Grand Rapids: Baker, 1978).

23. Ivan J. Kauffman, *He Was Here* (Grand Rapids: Brazos/Baker, 2000).

24. Martin Nystrom, "As the Deer," *Songs 4 Worship*, ed. Bill Wolaver and David Thibodeaux (USA: Time Life Music, 2001), 6–10.

25. Michael P. Green, *Illustrations for Biblical Preaching* (Grand Rapids: Baker, 1991), 53.

26. Orel Hershiser with Jerry B. Jenkins, *Out of the Blue* (Brentwood, Tenn.: Wolgemuth & Hyatt, 1989), 206.
27. Ibid., 208.
28. Ibid., 208.
29. Sauna Winsor, "When Charlie Sings," in *Stories for the Extreme Teen's Heart,* ed. Alice Grey (Sisters, Ore.: Multnomah, 2000), 156–157.
30. Fanny J. Crosby, "Blessed Assurance," composed by Phoebe P. Knapp, in *101 Hymn Stories,* ed. Kenneth K. Osbeck (Grand Rapids: Kregel, 1997), 43.
31. Ibid., 42.
32. Roy B. Zuck, *The Speaker's Quote Book* (Grand Rapids: Kregel, 1997), 380.
33. Nancy Leigh DeMoss, "Gratitude and Humility," *Decision Magazine*, Billy Graham Evangelistic Association, October 1, 2009, http://www.billygraham.org/articlepage.asp?articleid=1125
34. Michael P. Green, *Illustrations for Biblical Preaching* (Grand Rapids: Baker, 1991), 120.
35. David B. Smith, *The Voice of Prophecy*, December 15, 2000, http://www.vop.com/previous_broadcasts/2000/december_2000/00506.
36. Johnson Oatman, Jr., "*Count Your Blessings*," composed by Edwin O. Excell, in *101 Hymn Stories,* ed. Kenneth K. Osbeck (Grand Rapids: Kregel, 1997), 54.
37. Kent Hughes, *John: That You May Believe* (Wheaton, Ill.: Crossway, 1999), 384.
38. Andrea Bocelli and Céline Dion, "The Prayer," *Sogno,* CD, Phillips B0000016X2.
39. Ibid.
40. "China-Sichuan-earthquake—Presentation Transcript," http://www.slideshare.net/yumengli/chinasichuanearthquake
41. Claire Cloninger and Don Moen, "I Offer my Life," in *Hosanna New Songs Collection 2* (Taiwan: Eleim Christian Bookstore, 2000), 182.
42. Jim Burns, *Uncommon Stories & Illustrations* (Ventura, Calif.: Gospel Light, 2008), 101.

INDEX

SCRIPTURE INDEX

WinePressPublishing
Great Books, Defined.

To order additional copies of this book call:
1-877-421-READ (7323)
or please visit our website at
www.WinePressbooks.com

If you enjoyed this quality custom-published book,
drop by our website for more books and information.

www.winepresspublishing.com
"Your partner in custom publishing."